D.J.Dodds
March 1994

Grounds for Change

Grounds for Change

Major Gardens of the Twentieth Century

William Howard Adams

Principal Photography by
Everett H. Scott

A Bulfinch Press Book
Little, Brown and Company

Boston • Toronto • London

Half-title: **Paley Park,
Zion and Breen Associates**

Frontispiece: **Stonypath, Ian Hamilton Finlay**

Text copyright © 1993 by William Howard Adams

Color photographs copyright © 1993 Everett H. Scott

Photographs on pages 132–137 copyright © 1993 Michael Moran

Photograph on pages 198–199 copyright © 1989 Peter Mauss/Esto

First Edition

Adams, William Howard
        Grounds for change: major gardens of the twentieth century /
William Howard Adams; principal photography by Everett H. Scott.–
1st ed.
          p. cm.
        "A Bulfinch Press book."
        Includes bibliographical references and index.
        ISBN 0-8212-1902-2
        1. Gardens–History–20th century. 2. Landscape architecture–
History–20th century. 3. Gardens–Pictorial works. 4. Landscape
architecture–Pictorial works. 5. Landscape architects. I. Scott, Everett. II. Title.
SB465.A33 1993
712'.092'2–dc20   92–22122

Bulfinch Press is an imprint and trademark of Little, Brown and Company (Inc.)
Published simultaneously in Canada by Little, Brown & Company (Canada) Limited

Designed by Sametz Blackstone Associates
Imagesetting in Berthold Akzidenz Grotesk by Graphics Express

PRINTED IN SINGAPORE

Contents

Preface

Of all the arts—painting, sculpture, music, architecture, dance, theater, even that arriviste, photography—only landscape design has been denied an account of its history and achievements produced in the twentieth century. While it is by no means an unknown domain as some have claimed, critics and historians have ignored the subject. This very neglect might suggest that the discipline has fallen so far behind the other art forms in its aesthetic and cultural significance that it has earned its low estate. I intend to challenge that conclusion.

If the making of gardens and the organization of the landscape have, in different cultures throughout history, represented and served in complex ways the larger world in which they exist, as John Dixon Hunt has reminded us, their history and importance as cultural objects exemplifying the modern world could not have all but vanished in this century as the meager written record might suggest. Just as the critics and art historians embrace and somehow account for painters as diverse as Picasso, Twombly, and Rothko, so the equally eclectic, rich, and seemingly discontinuous work of major garden designers must be recognized as having claim on some aspect of modern sensibility.

In the case of garden design lumped together with the other arts, an obvious caveat must be reiterated. The concept of an avant-garde—working at the edge of, and fueling change in, an experimental, ephemeral way—doesn't serve this field of slow evolution, constrained by its symbiotic relationship with nature, a condition that does not pertain to the other arts. The very materials and conditions of garden making separate it from, say, painting and sculpture, where the artist has to think of something new every year. The element of time required for a garden to mature into the form its designer conceived at the outset also separates it from architecture, where fashions come and go with the speed of change in the couturier's salon. Maybe gardens are closer to poems; I am reminded of the poet James Merrill's remark that he never saw a poem that he couldn't "relate to something fifty years old, if not two hundred."

The claim of a cultural context as theoretical justification for any of the arts seems obvious, and the ability to see and appraise man's calculated intervention into space for both practical and aesthetic reasons has been the foundation of garden history. But the more distant past in every field of the arts is easier to deal with according to accepted documents, formulas, labels, and an agreed-upon body of work created by recognized artists. Since there is very little in the way of an existing pantheon of twentieth-century landscape designers to appraise or a canonical body of work to be accepted or challenged, the preliminary mapping that I have attempted has been both exhilarating and daunting. Like any pioneer I have had to carry out the work through firsthand examination, taking me on many exotic field trips over several years to see and experience directly any likely candidate.

Landscape design, garden design, or garden art (I consider the subject broad enough to employ all these labels without going into distinctions) cannot be left solely to photographic documentation in the way that art historians can treat paintings, sculpture, and even architecture. The three-dimensional quality of space and the viewer's movement through space sets up a dynamic that cannot be reduced to a symbolic color slide, as in the case of a painting.

For the purpose of a book, the camera has to be relied upon, and in this the work of Everett Scott, using the incomparable but difficult 8 x 10 view camera, has been a major element in capturing the subject for a large audience. This led to the other basic qualification—that of survival. The subject must have survived in reasonably good photogenic quality. Many key works of the century have disappeared, and where possible, contemporary illustrations have been included in the introductory essay.

Grounds for Change

At the beginning of the twentieth century, opinions on the future of the garden were as divided as predictions on the future of painting, architecture, or the ballet. Passions could stir partisan action if not war. For Dr. Joachim Carvallo, wealthy scientist, garden aesthete, and owner of a dilapidated château in the Loire region called Villandry, the new layout of a garden in 1904 could still deliver a political, even theological message that some might have considered subversive. After marrying an American heiress, Dr. Carvallo was ready to build what would become the finest model of an ideal French Renaissance garden on the old terraces of the château, since all traces of the original garden had disappeared. It was time, the Spanish doctor decided, to declare war on Jean-Jacques Rousseau's philosophy manifest in the fashionable *jardin anglais* that had persisted in France for more than a century. Such gardens in the English manner, replacing the relics of the ancien régime following the Revolution, had reached a climax during the reign of Napoleon III. But even in their modified French version, the loose improvisations of their composition clearly represented to Dr. Carvallo an assault on sound Roman Catholic doctrine and civic order. The relaxed lines of English gardens expressed, he declared, "the principles of an absurd egalitarianism contrary to nature and good sense."[1] Villandry, in its newly revived geometric order inspired by the sixteenth-century plans of the French architect and engraver Jacques Androuet Du Cerceau (c. 1515/20–c. 1584), its avenue of limes and patterned squares planted out in herbs and vegetables mixed with flowers, would serve as exemplar to gardeners confused both in garden design and in matters of faith.

The doctor's contemporary, the distinguished architect Sir Reginald Blomfield (1856–1942), also detected something unsettling in what he viewed as the indulgent inventions of the new natural school of "landscape gardeners," although hidden political issues may not have been a part of Blomfield's agenda. But the absence of any articulated alternative to what he considered a pernicious failure of modern garden design to establish any firm principles was indeed alarming. So he, too, had come down firmly on the side of order in the landscape a decade earlier than Dr. Carvallo when he published his passionate polemic *The Formal*

1. Jellicoe et al., p. 589.

Irwin Miller Residence,
Dan Kiley
(see pages 148–151)

The garden at Pitmidden, Aberdeenshire, as illustrated by F. Inigo Thomas, in Reginald Blomfield's *The Formal Garden in England*.

Garden in England (1892). Blomfield's structured formula was not so much a defense of the social establishment, but rather the rational extension of his architectural training based on tested principles. "The question at issue is a very simple one," he declared at the outset. "Is the garden to be considered in relation to the house, and as an integral part of design which depends for its success on the combined effect of house and garden; or is the house to be ignored in dealing with the garden?"[2] The answer became self-evident as he warmed to his theme. "The formal [so labeled by its ill-wishers] treatment of the garden ought…to be called the architectural treatment of gardens, for it consists in the extension of the principles of design which govern the house to the grounds that surround it."[3]

Frederick Law Olmsted (1822–1903), the founder of the new American profession of landscape architecture, was in London in 1892 when the debate over what Blomfield and his opponents, led by William Robinson, believed to be the future of garden design was at its height. "A complete return to the old formal gardening is to be desired rather than the present contradictory hash of formal-natural gardening should continue," the creator of Central Park noted in one of his few remembered observations on design theory. "The tendency to formality is very strong here, and as for a true natural style, I see nothing in it."[4] Olmsted was working at the time with the architect Richard Morris Hunt, who had been commissioned to design Biltmore, a monumental French Renaissance château begun in 1891 for George Vanderbilt's estate in North Carolina. Biltmore represented the beginning of a notable era that would continue until the Depression brought an end to it in the 1930s. For both architecture and landscape setting, the Great American Estate Era would be dominated by the distinctive American interpretation of the Ecole des Beaux-Arts precepts of architecture-symmetry, balance, and hierarchy that flowed naturally from and were dominated by the architecture itself. In its cultivated, classical references to an established past, it was a system that was comforting to a newly rich and unsure clientele eager to emulate European fashion.

2. Blomfield, p. 1.

3. Ibid., p. 2.

4. Quoted in Jellicoe et al., p. 409.

With unimagined wealth pouring into the centers of American capitalism, the extravagant possibilities for house and garden seemed limitless, especially if they were orchestrated by firms like McKim, Mead and White, Carrère and Hastings, or Delano and Aldrich. Talented in the new eclectia and the politics of taste, these firms were capable of delivering a complete estate package of house, gardens, grounds, swimming pools, polo fields, stables, Italianate terraces, or whatever fancy the client might desire. New construction and earth-moving technology enabled work to be accomplished in record time and before a mercurial patron or his wife could change his or her mind. Avenues of full-grown trees could be quickly moved into place, exotic plants gathered from halfway around the world, and lakes created in a desert with breathtaking speed. At Biltmore, Olmsted laid out a romantic winding road leading through four thousand acres of pastoral mountain scenery up to the 365-room mansion. Around the house itself, elaborate formal gardens were created. Blomfield would have called it a triumphant "affair of a dominant idea which stamps its impress on house and grounds alike."[5]

5. Blomfield, p. 3.

American estate gardens at the turn of the century drew widely from the garden traditions of Italy, France, and England. Books and magazines illustrating princely vestiges of the seventeenth and eighteenth centuries, particularly those from Italy, were eagerly collected by parvenue connoisseurs. Many of the architects and artists had studied abroad and, like Charles A. Platt (1861–1933), who was studying landscape painting, were captivated by Italian villa gardens. While Platt was in Europe, he wrote a small but influential book on the subject, one of the first of a series to be written by American enthusiasts. Platt's book and his subsequent articles on the Italian villa published by *Harper's* magazine opened up all kinds of professional opportunities when he returned to establish his practice as an estate designer par excellence. By looking to the European past for inspiration, Platt, like Reginald Blomfield, believed he had found a useful tool for applying critical analysis to modern landscape design and a method for once again uniting architecture and the designed landscape. He also found in the image of villa and garden that essential element of escape demanded by rich and often insecure

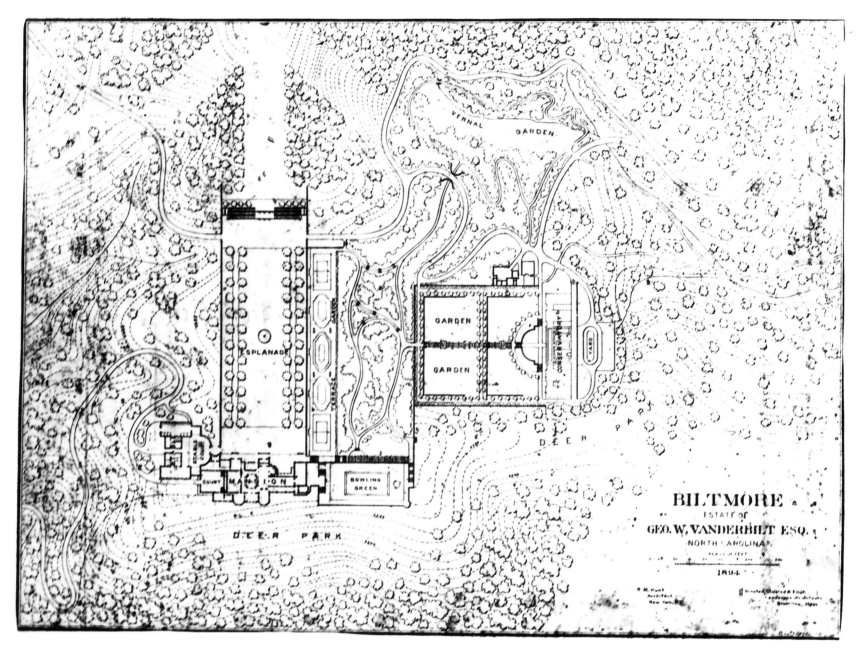

Frederick Law Olmsted plan for Biltmore (1894)
(Courtesy of the Frances Loeb Library,
Graduate School of Design, Harvard University)

American patrons. If they had not seen the real thing, Maxfield Parrish's misty paintings were more than adequate. Platt's most celebrated commission, that for the villa on Lake Michigan of Harold F. McCormick, heir to a farm-machinery fortune, achieved notoriety when it replaced Frank Lloyd Wright's original proposal. Platt's Italian grammar of design, incorporating references to Villa Lante, the Villa Farnese at Caprarola, and the Villa d'Este projected the right cultivated tone for his midwestern patrons, who had been convinced by the designer that the Illinois landscape was really a piece of Tuscany.[6]

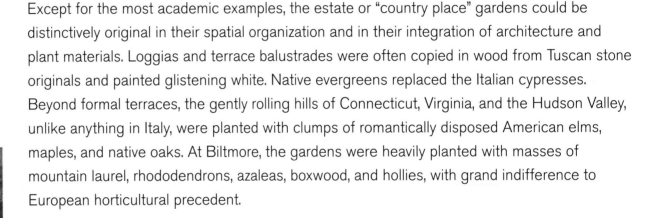

6. *American Renaissance, 1876–1917*, p. 85.

Except for the most academic examples, the estate or "country place" gardens could be distinctively original in their spatial organization and in their integration of architecture and plant materials. Loggias and terrace balustrades were often copied in wood from Tuscan stone originals and painted glistening white. Native evergreens replaced the Italian cypresses. Beyond formal terraces, the gently rolling hills of Connecticut, Virginia, and the Hudson Valley, unlike anything in Italy, were planted with clumps of romantically disposed American elms, maples, and native oaks. At Biltmore, the gardens were heavily planted with masses of mountain laurel, rhododendrons, azaleas, boxwood, and hollies, with grand indifference to European horticultural precedent.

The Harold F. McCormick house and gardens, viewed from Lake Michigan.

The absence in the American landscape of the inevitable well-worn look and feel brought about by time, which was so obvious to European visitors and the more sophisticated Americans like Henry James (who complained about the dearth of ruins), was even more apparent in the first garden creations of Newport, Long Island, Chicago, California, and other centers of new economic power. There was no way that the proud property owner could acquire the telltale marks of centuries for his jumped-up establishment that had been created as an ensemble by the architect and his landscape designer in a matter of months, or at most a few years. Even when instant patinas were attempted, as Addison Mizner tried on some of his Florida extravaganzas, no one was fooled.

Villa Vizcaya's Casba under construction
(Vizcaya Museum and Gardens—Archives)

**View of the waterway through the hammock
to the Casba at Villa Vizcaya**
(Vizcaya Museum and Gardens—Archives)

Another characteristic that distinguished the American estate garden, as Malcolm Cairns has pointed out, was the bold way in which "the spatial hierarchies in [the] architecture were transferred directly to the garden and landscape. Loggias and porches opened to outdoor formal terraces. Central foyers and halls extended to outdoor vistas through formal lawns, parterres or water cascades." This is of course basic Beaux Arts doctrine, but the more flamboyant use of native trees—oaks, elms, maples, evergreens—in allées and parks underlined the architectonic qualities of the layout, distinguishing it in scale, color, and mass from its European ancestry.[7]

7. Tischler, p. 133.

Architectural books published in Europe had exercised a growing influence on the course of American architecture in the eighteenth and nineteenth centuries. Similarly, imported garden books using photographic reproductions to document the historic garden traditions of Italy and England played a significant role in shaping American garden tastes at the turn of the twentieth century, especially with the advent of photographic reproduction. In 1900, H. Inigo Triggs (1876–1923) produced *Formal Gardens in England and Scotland* to illustrate with photographs and plans the thesis advanced by Reginald Blomfield. *The Art and Craft of Garden Making*, by Thomas H. Mawson (1861–1933) appeared in five editions between 1900 and 1926. As the title indicates, Mawson's book was influenced by the Arts and Crafts movement in perfecting an impressive skill in linking house and garden. Between 1899 and 1908 Gertrude Jekyll (1843–1932) published no fewer than eight popular volumes. *Country Life*, the English weekly publication, may not have been widely circulated in America but its influence in the British Isles was enormous. Books such as *Garden Ornament* (1918), by Miss Jekyll, published by the magazine, had a considerable but not always successful impact on the postwar gardens of the 1920s, especially in the new neo-Georgian gardens on both sides of the Atlantic. Statues, columns, and urns were imported or copied from European models but their new settings often ignored the scale, color, and texture of the original disposition. Sir Edwin Lutyens (1869–1944), who often worked with Jekyll before the First World War, freely translated from history, but with an originality that lifted the results above the self-conscious

Lutyens's Mughal Garden, part of the
Viceregal complex in New Delhi, looking west
from the Viceroy's House.
(Irving, *Indian Summer: Lutyens, Baker and
Imperial Delhi*, Yale University Press)

pastiche that often results from wholesale rummaging in the fashionable past. The gardens of Lutyens and Jekyll, dictated by Lutyens's architecture, reflected distinctly English domestic traditions of building and gardening idioms found in old farmsteads, villages, and country homes, disguising Lutyens's underlying hierarchies of formal design principles that nevertheless allowed him to exploit existing rustic English settings created over the centuries. It was a part of the famous partnership's romantic ideal. In the years following World War I, he moved on to his imperial Palladian style, culminating in the monumental buildings of the new capital of India at New Delhi. The garden for the viceroy's house was built in 1917 and was inspired by the strict geometry of sixteenth-century Mughal gardens. The garden is dominated by the use of water far more lavish than any Mughal emperor could command. English borders and lawns are integrated without ethnic or religious concern. The results are brilliant.

In the more rigorous application of architectural principles linking the house to the garden, particularly when classical rules were followed, the architecture often dominated the results, something the Lutyens-Jekyll partnership managed to avoid. Historically this architectural unity seemed to be confirmed by the evidence found in surviving European gardens extending back to the Renaissance. Yet for architects and garden designers trained in the Beaux Arts tradition, the lessons modified and transformed by time were not always clearly understood. Literal translation of Mediterranean gardens into the North American or English environment of different climate and soil conditions could result in an awkward hodgepodge.

The subtle fusion of art and nature was identified as the supreme achievement of the Italian garden by the American novelist Edith Wharton when she published *Italian Villas and Their Gardens* in 1904. Because she believed that modern gardeners had much to learn from the spirit and fundamental principles of the Italian models, it was necessary to explain in some detail precisely what could and what could not be learned from garden styles of the past. The first thing that must be kept in mind, she wrote, was to understand that such gardens could not be copied, as some Americans were attempting. "The cult of the Italian garden has spread

The theater at La Palazzina, Siena. Illustration by Maxfield Parrish for Edith Wharton's *Italian Villas and Their Gardens*

from England to America," she noted with some concern, "and there is a general feeling that, by placing a marble bench here and a sun-dial there, Italian 'effects' may be achieved." But if their true lesson was to be understood, Italian gardens in all their variety could only "be copied, not in the letter but in the spirit."[8] A few years before the publication of *The Italian Garden*, Wharton's niece Beatrix Jones [Farrand], in preparation for a career as a landscape architect, or, as she preferred to call herself, a "landscape gardener," traveled widely in Europe and studied firsthand all the Italian gardens. While Farrand's later work in America would often be quite formal in character, reflecting her early investigations, she nevertheless understood her aunt's dictum that any influence had to be absorbed and translated in an "impressionist manner."[9] Dumbarton Oaks is an outstanding example of her impressionistic, well-bred interpretation of historical European sources adapted to an American setting.

Before she returned to the United States to begin her practice and to participate in the launching of the American Society of Landscape Architects, Beatrix Jones had also gone to England, where she met Gertrude Jekyll and saw some of her work. She was particularly impressed with the old "confirmed and renewed" Tudor gardens at Penshurst, in Kent, which Jekyll also admired. Jekyll's technique of softening architectural lines of the walks and terraces with subtle, impressionistic borders encouraged by her friend and mentor William Robinson also impressed the young American. It is difficult to be precise about Jekyll's other contributions in her later collaborations with Lutyens beyond her carefully worked out planting schemes. What cannot be in doubt is the influence of her now mythic herbaceous border and with it, as Joseph Rykwert has pointed out, the image of the garden chatelaine appropriately attired and actually working in the garden rather than merely looking at it. Gardening throughout the Western world was no longer a spectator sport. "She participated, *tu per tu* with vegetable nature in the creation of her environment."[10]

Jekyll, Robinson, and Lutyens have all been associated with the principles of the Arts and Crafts movement led by the poet and designer William Morris (1834–1896). As Deborah Nevins

8. Wharton, p. 12.

9. Balmori, McGuire, and Peck, p. 24.

10. Rykwert, n.p.

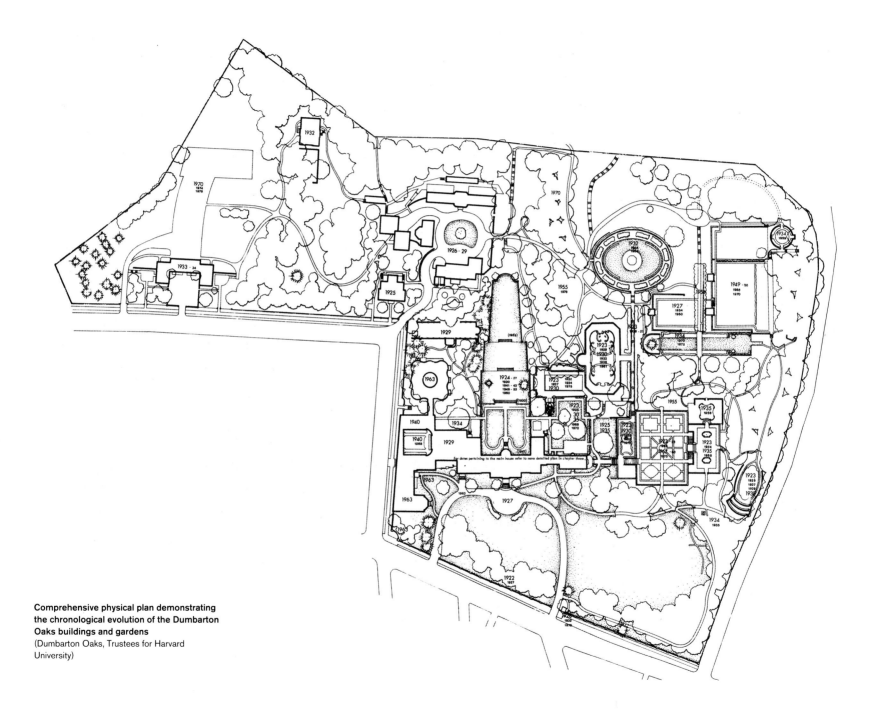

**Comprehensive physical plan demonstrating
the chronological evolution of the Dumbarton
Oaks buildings and gardens**
(Dumbarton Oaks, Trustees for Harvard
University)

has pointed out in her introduction to the 1984 edition of Robinson's *The English Flower Garden*, Robinson and his followers never called themselves Arts and Crafts garden designers. But Morris, who had picked up on the garden design debate between Robinson and Sir Reginald Blomfield, supported Robinson's advocacy of a return to simplicity as a means of reforming the overdesigned Victorian garden. This revolt, as Nevins documents, had been in the works for years and reached back to 1838, when Ruskin's *Poetry of Architecture* had just appeared. Robinson's and later Jekyll's ideals more accurately drew on this background and paralleled these ideals of the Arts and Crafts movement as an important source of inspiration.

Robinson's strong defense of the so-called "wild garden" and the natural landscape seemed to suggest that he rejected all use of architectural principles or architectural accessories. Neither Jekyll nor Lutyens intended to be drawn into the cul de sac of this debate. Just as Robinson's passionate polemics on behalf of all English garden values profoundly appealed to the new collaborators, F. Inigo Thomas's illustration of the Blomfield examples drawn from the garden settings of Canons Ashby, Pitmidden, and other old English gardens, suggested a resolution to the argument and a common ground for architects and gardeners.

Lutyens as an architect had drawn particular creative strength from nature, following the examples of the English architect A. W. N. Pugin and Ruskin, who had advanced a compelling argument for designers to return to basic sources for sustenance. Both nature and traditional craftsmen who understood nature's qualities by working directly with it could offer cultural and aesthetic redemption in the face of spreading industrialized degradation that promised to engulf rural England. Ruskin's reverence for nature, combined with his High Anglican sympathies, carried Rousseau's moral idealism into a world of medieval make-believe by the end of the century. But Ruskin's Gothic, anticlassical sentiments turned out to be just as stifling as the worn-out conventions of the Renaissance. It was, as critic and landscape architect Christopher Tunnard remarked, hardly conducive to artistic progress. The Arts and Crafts movement did see in Ruskin's polemics a useful strategy to attack the ugliness and squalor of mass production brought on by the Industrial Revolution, but Ruskin's Gothic Revival was not a living style for the new society Morris and his followers envisioned. On the other hand, William Robinson's constant theme of naturalism and informality, combined with his appreciation of the vernacular garden of the English cottage, epitomized the horticultural reaction to the artificial eclecticism in architecture and design identified by Morris as a sign of a sick society.

By the end of the first decade of the twentieth century, the debate between the Formal and the Natural schools of garden design, as framed by Blomfield and Robinson, had run its course. In Lutyens's enlargement of the fifteenth-century manor house at Great Dixter, in Sussex, for Nathaniel Lloyd, and the work at Hestercombe, in Somerset, his first collaboration with Jekyll, the conflict had become jaded and was perceived as no longer relevant. Hestercombe displays Lutyens's careful work in the details of steps, walks, and pools. He rephrased Blomfield's classical formula when he said that "every garden scheme should have a backbone, a central idea beautifully phrased. Every wall, path, stone, and flower should have its relationship to the central idea."[11] But Lutyens's results were far different. With the utmost sympathy for materials, the texture of the past in old manor houses and farm buildings, a sensitivity for the site and ordinary rural surroundings, Lutyens found new ways to unite the architecture and the garden. Just as Wharton had insisted on the study of the Italian Renaissance villa garden, and Dr. Carvallo sought salvation in the sixteenth-century engravings of French gardens, Lutyens and Jekyll had carefully absorbed the lessons of the past found in modest rectories, derelict Tudor farm buildings, and simple roadside cottages.

In 1900, Edward Hudson, founder of *Country Life*, commissioned Lutyens to design his new house, called The Deanery. Lutyens, now collaborating with his partner "Miss Bumps," as he affectionately called Jekyll, was able to demonstrate in his original design how irrelevant the either/or formal/informal issue had become. Ian Phillips's description of The Deanery cannot be improved upon:

11. Quoted in Jellicoe et al., p. 173.

An old, high, brick wall forms the roadside boundary; a small gate through it opens into a wide, vaulted passageway to the front door, with arched openings to a paved fountain-court on one side, and to a small formal garden on the other. Straight through the house is the garden doorway in a deep embrasure arch; this gives on to a broad terrace which prolongs the axial line further, towards a generous flight of semi-circular steps. Here formality gives way to rough-mown grass rides through the trees of the old orchard.[12]

12. Ibid., p. 136.

In England and in America, as well as on the Continent, industrialism had brought about enormous transformations of the older, settled landscape and its denizens. It had also quickly produced a new class of rich businessmen anxious to disguise themselves in the trappings of the established gentry they were beginning to replace. Middle-class English industrialists, once they had succeeded, bought or built a house in the country, wore Barbour jackets and Wellington boots, shot pheasant, rode to hounds, and more often than not, thanks to the advances of science and technology, gardened on an international scale inconceivable to earlier generations. Some of the new technology that had made the fortunes—oil, the internal-combustion engine, construction—made the work easier and faster. Maintenance itself was mechanized with new mowing equipment and irrigation. If the entrepreneur was daring enough to build his estate from scratch, Blomfield and Lutyens were ready to oblige. Both architects specialized in adapting the earlier architectural styles to a new breed of client, providing more functional modifications for their houses and grounds that appealed to the gentry-tycoons. Lutyens's grasp of time-honored materials and building crafts, which he employed in his understated ensembles, reflected an original interpretation of vernacular traditions. The eclectic combinations of French and Italian elements seen in Blomfield's Edwardian establishments were influenced, no doubt, by his academic research into French and Italian architectural history.

Two national institutions created in the last decades of the nineteenth century—the National Trust and *Country Life* magazine—were to have a significant influence on garden fashions in Great Britain throughout the twentieth century. The National Trust was created in 1895 out of a growing concern for the preservation of the historic fabric of the threatened countryside and its vast, stately establishments, which were being undermined by economic and social upheavals. The country-house estates that were passed to the Trust often included major gardens, usually of a historic character that had to be protected along with the architecture.

In 1887, *Country Life* was founded as a magazine dedicated to the preservation of "country" values in all their manifestations and eccentricities. Lutyens's work was regularly featured and illustrated, advancing a broad appreciation of his achievements along with Jekyll's before World War I. The magazine also featured works of many other garden designers, documenting their work with photographs and often comprehensive descriptions. In addition to the National Trust and *Country Life*, the Royal Horticultural Society expanded its membership, encouraging a greater knowledge among amateur laymen. The society's experiments at Wisley garden, and its dissemination of horticultural research also grew in influence to expand the layman's appreciation of the horticultural riches that could be grown in Great Britain.

English garden design, like architecture, during the first half of the twentieth century reflected a state of uncertainty and lack of focus marked by the founding of a professional institute of landscape architecture in 1929. But the passionate, informed, amateur gardener, whose numbers were legion and growing, showed no apparent confusion. In 1909, the year that Thomas H. Mawson became the first lecturer in landscape design at the Liverpool University Department of Civic Design, the aristocrat Sir George Sitwell—writer, art collector, and gentleman gardener—outlined his own solution to the decline of the art of garden making. It was a solution that emphatically did not call for the services of trained landscape architects, as the members of the new institute called themselves. Sitwell's book *On the Making of Gardens* was a somewhat more personal and eccentric, though no less passionate, sequel to Sir Reginald Blomfield's call to hold firm to classical principles that had been tested by time. The garden maker must somehow return to the philosophy and skills of the Italian Quattrocento, where salvation would be found. "If the world is to make great gardens again," he announced, "we must discover and apply in the changed circumstances of modern life the principles which guided the makers of the Renaissance."[13]

13. Sitwell, p. xvi.

The creation of Hidcote Manor Garden by the American gardener and man of leisure Lawrence Johnston, begun around 1907, actually seemed to justify Sitwell's faith in a Florentine gardener reincarnate. Hidcote is a brilliant synthesis of horticultural sophistication and design concepts boldly taken from many garden traditions brought about by the genius of its owner. Its fame was well established long before it was given to the National Trust in 1948. In direct lineage both in its amateur origin and by its influence, is the garden of Sissinghurst Castle, created by Victoria Sackville-West (1892–1962) and her husband, Harold Nicolson (1886–1968). The influence of Sissinghurst, like Hidcote's, was institutionalized in 1962 when it also came under the protection of the Trust, who opened it to the public hardly thirty years after the Nicolsons first cleared debris from the derelict castle ruin they had discovered in the Kent countryside.

For knowledgeable Americans looking for a gardening past at the beginning of the century, George Washington and Thomas Jefferson represented the native amateur gardener par excellence in the English tradition of the eighteenth century. But the elegant examples established by these founding fathers on their slave-powered estates in Virginia were difficult to follow or to emulate in the restless, wayward modern industrialized world. The forces of material conquest, civil disorder, and national expansion carried forward by the new waves of energetic immigrants anxious to be a part of the action relegated the memory of Mount Vernon and Monticello to ancient history. It was not until 1916, in fact, when Fiske Kimball wrote his landmark article "Thomas Jefferson, Landscape Architect," followed by the publication of his drawings, that Jefferson's original contributions to landscape design were accurately documented and recognized.

By the end of the nineteenth century, the new cities that had sprung up overnight across the American continent were ready to "bring order out of chaos," in the words of the Chicago architects Daniel Burnham and Edward H. Bennett.[14] They were the words of the battle hymn of the evangelical City Beautiful movement, demanding a new civic sense of public grandeur in the country's architecture, parks, gardens, and city planning. Fine arts commissions, civic leagues, and planning societies suddenly appeared. Schemes for new parks, avenues, and public gardens materialized, in elegant drawings, from Kansas City and Denver to the latest American colony, the Philippines. The vision of the future was dominated by architecture, so long as its genealogy could be stretched to reach back to classical roots.

The City Beautiful movement and its impact on urban design stem from a complex and distinctly American impulse beyond the scope of this narrative. As a dramatic model for architecture and landscape design, however, the influential World's Columbian Exposition, which opened on the shores of Lake Michigan in 1893, was a crystallization of City Beautiful ideals. It delivered a powerful message through its architecture and landscape, "to celebrate patriotism, inculcate morals and to stand as the visible concrete symbol of high endeavor."[15] John Charles Olmsted (1852–1920), a senior partner of his father's firm, which had worked on the Exposition, told the American Institute of Architects in an address in 1900 that public buildings and their setting in America must conform to classicism's formula of order and beauty. They must be "strongly formal whether they are perfectly symmetrical or not, and this formal quality ought to be recognized in the plan of their surroundings if the total effect is to be consistent."[16]

14. *American Renaissance*, p. 21.

15. Ibid.

16. Ibid., p. 84.

Henry Adams thought he detected a great historical truth in the classical stage sets created by Richard Morris Hunt, Daniel Burnham, Frederick Law Olmsted, and the other artists, architects, and landscape designers who had brought about the shimmering unity of the Exposition. They had, Adams wrote with uncharacteristic optimism, "leaped directly from Corinth and Syracuse and Venice, over the heads of London and New York, to impose classical standards on plastic Chicago."[17]

17. *The Education of Henry Adams,* quoted in *American Renaissance,* p. 28.

The long shadows cast by the imperial facades decorating the shore of Lake Michigan did not take long to reach the nation's capital along the Potomac. Adams's use of the word "leap" became, in fact, a better metaphor than "shadow" when Daniel Burnham, as a result of his orchestration of the Columbian Exposition, was named head of the newly formed Commission of Fine Arts in Washington, D.C., established to redesign the Mall. This new body was to take up the work originally envisioned by Senator James McMillan's Senate Park Commission, formed in 1901–1902 to set the design course for a monumental capital city. "It is the general opinion," McMillan wrote, "that for monumental work, Greece and Rome furnish the styles of architecture best adapted to serve the manifold wants of today, not only as to beauty and dignity, but as to utility."[18] A number of architects like Burnham, whose careers became that of impresario planners, also began to see their new mission in the guise of city planning. It was an opportunity to extend their practical, organizing skills over the entire man-made landscape encompassing parks, road systems, and public gardens with their educational and entertainment facilities. The professional recognition of city planning was timely as undeveloped countryside was fed at an alarming rate into the urban network of expansion, becoming grist for the city planning mill. This organized vision of the totally planned urban landscape, like the totally planned private estate, was a dominant force in all aspects of design for American cities throughout much of the twentieth century. Garden design as an art form, reflecting the unpredictable, experimental vitality of the Modern movement had little appeal for a new generation of landscape architects and civil engineers instilled with well-worn ideals first laid down in Henry Adams's Corinth and Syracuse.

18. *American Renaissance,* p. 12.

City planning was not a phenomenon limited to the United States. Around the year 1900, as historian Richard Guy Wilson has pointed out, there seemed to be a "simultaneous explosion of interest and concern for the physical and aesthetic conditions in Austria, France, Germany, Spain and England." The dramatic growth of old cities in industrial countries was both disturbing and challenging. "The rotting of cities' older cores and industrial sectors, and the desire…to give an artistic dimension to cities and improve the living environment" stirred politicians, businessmen, philanthropists, and artists.[19]

19. Ibid., p. 87.

In 1917, Thomas Mawson wrote a report on what he believed to be the future of landscape architecture in Britain.[20] Prepared for an American audience, Mawson's essay held out the hope that "landscape architecture" would soon embrace the entire environment both in appreciation and in the studies of the subject, then only just beginning in British universities. His vision was as large as that of American and continental city planners, aggressively reaching out, in his words, to take in "the architecture of extended areas" of the expanding cities. He went even further and proposed that the phrase should be included in the definition of the term "landscape architecture," a label that had uneasily replaced the earlier "landscape garden." "At the present time landscape architecture in England is slowly waking from lethal slumbers into which the whole art descended under the mistaken ideals of the late Georgian and early Victorian period." But in both the energetic, pragmatic drive of American city planning and in fulfilling the broad aims envisioned by Mawson, the field seemed to move further away from articulating any clear theories of landscape architecture and garden design. As Steven Krog has written, "the wide range of environmental, planning, and design issues" that evolved precipitated a shift in the center of gravity of the profession, a shift creating "an imbalance of collective ideological will" leading to a crisis of self-doubt by the end of the century.[21]

20. Mawson, p. 113.

21. Krog, "Whither the Garden," p. 94.

The seventeenth-century parks and gardens of France are taken for granted as a part of that nation's cultural and topographical patrimony. It is a heritage of style and form that even in the twentieth century never seems far from the surface of landscape design or city planning, masking whatever professional self-doubt there might be. In recent decades, for example, the stretching of the old axis of the Tuileries garden running from the Louvre to the new office park of skyscrapers at La Défense seems a quintessentially French gesture. The intellectual rigor of Bernard Tschumi's point grid that conceptually underpins the Parc de La Villette on the northwest edge of Paris could not have failed to communicate to its municipal sponsors in 1983 a reasoned message of rigorous design reaching back to the grand traditions of Boyceau, Mollet, and Le Nôtre.

One of the essential elements of the French garden tradition has been its commitment to structure. Even in the nineteenth century, when Gabriel Thouin (1747–1829) and others formulated a rationalized version of Humphry Repton's approach to design, there remained a strong underlying form and rigid formula that was contrary to the intuitive, pragmatic improvisation of English garden philosophy or the later energy of American city planners. Although many of the royal parks of the ancien régime had incorporated a fashionable *jardin anglais* into their formal systems of design before the Revolution, the original outlines were maintained. Napoleon's plan to transform Versailles into an English park never materialized, and by the 1850s the seventeenth-century gardens of the Duc du Maine at Sceaux were being restored along the lines first traced by Le Nôtre. Whether the accelerated interest in garden restoration during the decades following the bloody Commune of 1871 had political implications or was merely an inevitable cultural reaction, the return to the formal principles and visible order at the heart of French garden design was reassuring to a society that wanted to forget its revolutionary past of disordered violence.

Much of the modern restoration of French parks and gardens in the classic manner was carried out by the firm of Henri Duchêne (1841–1902) and his son Achille (1866–1947). Under their supervision André Le Nôtre's great masterpiece Vaux-le-Vicomte suddenly reemerged from the half-forgotten engravings of Israel Silvestre (1621–91) and the descriptions in court memoirs. The topographical exactness that the Duchênes were able to achieve is remarkable, setting a high standard for the twentieth-century phenomenon of garden restoration. Just before the First World War, Achille Duchêne completed the restoration of Courances, another relic of the ancien régime, to which he also successfully added a canal, ornamental basin, and small cascade that had not been a part of the original seventeenth-century scheme. His garden at Blenheim Palace, a completely original design for the ninth Duke of Marlborough, finished in 1930, is the finest example of the French classic style in Great Britain.

For some garden designers, especially on the Continent, the restorations of the Duchênes seemed to offer a source of inspiration. The recognition of garden design unified with the architecture as an art form imposed on nature in these historic relics of the Golden Age provided a new stimulus that was absent in the earlier romantic attempt to somehow re-create nature on its own terms. The pervasive Victorian jumble of styles was swept away with the return to a time-tested imposed order. Like the American Charles Platt and Edwin Lutyens in England, French landscape architects had also turned to history as a strategy to move beyond the eclecticism of the nineteenth century.

André Vera (fl. 1919–50) whose garden at Saint-Germain-en-Laye would be one of the first attempts to express the new ideas communicated by modern art in garden design, held serious reservations about the influence of historical precedent in the twentieth century. To him, it represented a useless illusion that had nothing to do with the modern world, a point he argued in an introduction to *Le Nouveau Jardin*, published in 1912. Even though he did not think that seventeenth-century revivals held the answer to contemporary design issues, he was unable to completely escape his classical heritage. His Sun Garden of 1919 on the Riviera was constructed on the most severe geometric lines and centered on a wide staircase flanked by cypresses leading down to the sea. In spite of Vera's reservations concerning the relevance of historical French precedent, there is the unmistakable mark of his French roots in the balanced organization of the *Jardin du Soleil*. There is, however, in its purity of form and the absence of decorative elements, a simplicity that would have been a sympathetic setting for a villa by the Viennese architect Josef Hoffmann. Ferdinand Bac, a French painter and landscape architect, had also found the Riviera climate and well-heeled clientele congenial. His own idiosyncratic investigation of the past established him as an early innovator in his design experiments with color, form, and materials. Born in 1859, he became a student of Mediterranean culture and traveled widely gathering "piles of annotations on the art of building as practiced in Latin countries."[22] He considered himself the founder of the revival of the Mediterranean school of gardening. The memories of half-forgotten villas, farmhouses, and terraced gardens of France, Italy, and Spain became his working notebook. "From all this memorabilia, which had lain dormant for so long, sprang the renewal of an architectural formula in which one will find everything but the hand of the architect….This is the architecture of sentiments…an art which builds upon our nostalgic reminiscences of places where we would have liked to set up our tent and remain, uplifted by Beauty and strengthened by Simplicity."[23] Bac's first work, in 1912, was a garden of Italian and Spanish inspiration designed for the Villa Croisset at Grasse, but his masterpiece is Les Colombières at Menton. His pictorial style at Les Colombières created a garden itinerary linking a number of traditions in the composition, bringing them "to life in order to relive the past,"[24] recalling Fletcher Steele's Naumkeag in Stockbridge, Massachusetts. Bac's most celebrated admirer was the Mexican Luis Barragán who, like Bac, was self-taught. "When one does not belong to any profession in particular," Bac once remarked, "nothing prevents one from becoming a landscape gardener."[25] While a young student in Mexico City, Barragán discovered Bac's writing and was deeply influenced by the Frenchman's philosophy and poetic reveries. Barragán's images of "the garden as a magic place for the enjoyment of meditation and companionship," in the words of Emilio Ambasz, paid homage in spirit to Bac.[26] Barragán's compositions have a strong theatrical quality, as Ambasz has pointed out. Bac's garden designs also have something of the static feeling of a stage set that no doubt appealed to the Mexican exploring the poetic images gathered in his own travels and more particularly from books.

22. Racine, Boursier-Mougenot, and Binet, p. 112.

23. Ibid.

24. Ibid.

25. Quoted in Racine, Boursier-Mougenot, and Binet, p. 110.

26. Ambasz, p. 105.

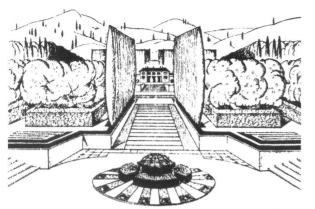

General view and plan for a Mediterranean garden, by André Vera, published in 1919 (Racine, Boursier-Mougenot, and Binet, *The Gardens of Provence and the French Riviera*, The MIT Press)

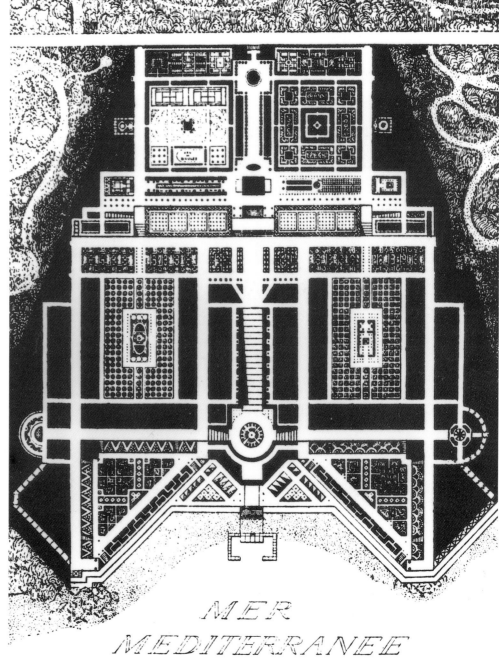

MER
MEDITERRANEE

**Sketch by Ferdinand Bac for the garden of
the Villa Croisset at Grasse**
(Racine, Boursier-Mougenot, and Binet, *The
Gardens of Provence and the French Riviera*,
The MIT Press)

Given the climate and indigenous horticultural traditions, spectacular gardens have always been possible along the Riviera. By the turn of the century, rich American and English patrons of the private garden along with fashionable Europeans were attracted there, followed by garden designers, many of them amateurs who created some major works. In 1892, Harold Peto (1854–1933) left a substantial practice of country house gardens in England and by 1900 had executed at least eight important and influential commissions on the Côte d'Azur. Like so many of his generation, Peto had been taken with Italian Renaissance gardens, and in his colonnaded pools, pavilions, stairs, and terraces, he managed to establish a balance and unity between the garden and the architecture that Sir George Sitwell and Edith Wharton would and did approve of. But within this nostalgic return to regional garden traditions, there were also experiments in the handling of space, and in the use of local, ordinary building materials and indigenous plants and trees.

There were other experiments in garden design, however, that were resolutely resistant to the seduction of the past, so attractive in a Mediterranean setting. In 1905–8, while he was a student in Brussels, the future architect Robert Mallet-Stevens watched the construction of his uncle's town house, the Palais Stoclet, which had been designed by Josef Hoffmann. Mallet-Stevens, who would himself later carry out significant experiments in modern garden design in Paris, was particularly impressed with Hoffmann's garden design for the Stoclet house, which had been integrated into the architecture without resorting to the usual historical references and decorations. Hoffmann had studied with Otto Wagner and was a member of the Vienna Secession when he founded the Wiener Werkstätte in 1903. This group of artists, architects, and craft workshops attempted to forge a link between art and industry on the order of the Arts and Crafts movement in England. The Palais Stoclet would be Hoffmann's greatest achievement, and Mallet-Stevens' reaction to it was "traumatic," according to Rykwert. This remarkable building linked Hoffmann's influence to later garden designers and architects whom Mallet-Stevens would himself inspire. The Stoclet house eludes precedents and comparisons and its alien, unfamiliar feeling extends into the garden composition itself, where nature has been sublimated into pure aesthetics. Located in the busy center of Brussels, the garden was conceived to provide complete privacy within its tall walls, consisting of masonry and hedges. The elementary, geometric forms Hoffmann used for the house are echoed in the organization of the garden spaces. The facade facing the garden, in turn, underlines its close relationship to the garden, reflecting a sympathetic symmetry in its composition. The axes of the house are at least partially continued into the garden by the rigid lines of classically regular trees and clipped hedges, providing a series of calculated views of the house framed by these plantings.

Within the decade in which the Palais Stoclet was being built in Brussels, events in Vienna signaled a hint of a turn in the direction architecture and garden design might take in the new century. In 1905, the architect Joseph M. Olbrich confirmed Hoffmann's resolute rejection of nature as a source of inspiration for the Stoclet house and garden. That year, in an address to landscape architects, Olbrich predicted that just as there were signs of a new architecture, a "new garden will also develop in our time, which will be in close relation and harmony" with the house.[27] In reaction to the English romanticism reflected in parks and gardens that had spread throughout the European landscape, Olbrich had created a mystical "garden of celestial colors" in Darmstadt, expressing his own cryptic sensibilities and new ideas. In his prescient remarks, given at a garden conference in Darmstadt in 1905, Olbrich offered a radical critique that the historical models of Italian, French, and English garden design could not supply. It was a criticism that would be repeated by André Vera in his rejection of historical revivals or reinterpretation. Rather, he called for *jardins "nouveaux," "modernes,"* and *"cubistes,"* later to be publicized by Mallet-Stevens. For Mallet-Stevens all aspects of design had to respond to the problems raised by modern architecture, even if nature had to be modified or even denatured in the process. "Why then, in a new world, with new and powerful components available, construct copies of old houses?"[28] Mallet-Stevens understood the radical new directions that Josef Hoffmann and the Wiener Werkstätte were opening up for art and design. By 1911, he was in command of his own design language: "Art is becoming simpler,

27. Olbrich, p. 13.

28. Quoted in Deshouliers et al., p. 36.

29. Quoted in Yvonne Brunhammer, "Robert Mallet-Stevens as Interior Architect," in Deshouliers et al., p. 111.

more sincere, banishing the petty decorative details, the triviality of over-abundant and irrational ornamentation," he wrote in an article on modern bathrooms.[29] "This rational architecture, where the construction is read, so to speak, where the component parts assert themselves frankly, in its turn transforms the other arts which derive from it: painting, sculpture and decoration evolve in the same direction and reveal new facets of themselves to us, more realistic, and as a result more ideal." In his "Lettres de Paris," published the same year in the Belgian magazine *Tekne*, he seems to recall the decorations and garden of the Palais Stoclet, although he doesn't mention it, or Hoffmann, when he applauds "the spreading use of clipped boxwood with its dark foliage outlined on light-coloured walls, the more widespread use in furnishings of white linen spangled with geometric drawings in black."[30]

30. Ibid., pp. 111–112.

Garden design seemed to discourage radical manifestos so prevalent in the other arts of the period, but there were one or two notable exceptions. "Garden art is the most notable and happiest negation of wild nature," Josef Lux declared in *Der Architekt* in 1909. "Art will create an antithesis to nature in the garden."[31] In the garden by Mallet-Stevens for the villa Les Roses Rouges, designed in 1914, the cross-axial composition and symmetrical ground planes follow traditional French design conventions reaching back to Du Cerceau, Dr. Carvallo's inspiration for the gardens at Villandry. The geometric lines of the plantings and aggressively stylized elements negated nature according to Lux's prediction five years earlier. Reinforced concrete, rarely seen in garden architecture, was used for the stairs and planting beds, while glass tile covered the electric lights illuminating the edge of the pool. But, as the critic Richard Wesley has observed, "nothing in the plan of the 'Roses Rouges,' however, represented a severe departure from established spatial and compositional traditions."

31. Lux, n.p.

The same was true of André Vera's design for a Mediterranean garden published in 1919. A small hemicycle enclosed with a trellised wall and topped with a clipped hedge, its stiff, stylized Viennese manner is an operatic caricature of Louis Seize motifs. The acclaim that Mallet-

Stevens and Vera received for their "*jardins d'avant-garde*," in fact should have been reserved for the small suburban garden Vera began a year later, in 1920, in collaboration with his brother Paul at Saint-Germain-en-Laye. Here, at last, was a garden that was equal to the rhetoric announcing the advent of "*le jardin Cubiste*." The trapezoidal space, as flat as a stretched canvas, was articulated with faceted, geometric parterres framed with white walks. The back wall was faced with panels of mirrors. It immediately attracted the contemporary eye of Man Ray, whose photograph is one of the few records of it to have survived.

The volatile, creative atmosphere of Paris when the young Mallet-Stevens first exhibited his drawings there, in 1912, conspired with the breakdown of traditional design hierarchies, with the result of encouraging the effort to elevate the aesthetics of garden design to the level of modern painting. The painter Frantz Jourdain, who had founded the annual Salon d'Automne in 1903, and the architect Anatole de Bardot believed passionately in the unity of all the arts. Through their efforts, architecture eventually became a special section of the Salon, providing a forum for the exchange of experimental ideas between young architects, artists, and designers.

In an article on the Salon, Mallet-Stevens praised Jourdain, who "admirably understood that in order to give new life to contemporary art, popularize it, make it appreciated, the public had to be given an exhibition which included all the disciplines covered by the arts, merging them together without arbitrary distinctions.…Painting, sculpture and decoration evolve in the same direction and reveal new facets of themselves to us, more realistic, and as a result more ideal."[32] Mallet-Stevens's own range of interests were diverse and large, encompassing in the Salon d'Automne of 1912 projects that ranged from concert halls and bathrooms to garden benches and park entrances.

32. Quoted in Brunhammer, p. 113.

After the war, the Salon as well as the atmosphere of experiment in Paris, now the unquestioned center of *l'esprit nouveau*, continued to attract artists and architects from

Europe and America. In 1925 the young Armenian émigré Gabriel Guevrékian moved to Paris from Vienna, where he had served as an apprentice of Josef Hoffmann. There he worked in the office of Mallet-Stevens, and both architects entered garden design projects in that year's Exposition des Arts Décoratifs. Mallet-Stevens's exhibition garden continued to explore the definition of volumes by the manipulation of ground planes and by applying contemporary motifs to traditional design. His reinforced-concrete trees were startling, expressing a strong commitment to new materials, yet the rectangular raised and depressed beds, also of concrete, betrayed a conventional approach to geometric composition.

Guevrékian's "*Jardin Persan*," a label given to it by the press, reached much further into the Cubist vocabulary of Braque and Picasso to create a completely original garden design. Richard Wesley has compared the little garden, which consisted of a triangular pool formed by four red and blue basins, with Picasso's *Man with a Mandolin* and has identified a number of similarities. "In each project the edges of the compositional field are given clear definition in order to separate the faceted object from its background. Within this field each artist attempts to dissolve perspective by presenting space as shallow and compressed and tilted forward into the pictorial plane. Both seem to emphasize volume and surface rather than mass through the use of faceted planes. Each appears to present these planes as transparent, interpenetrating and luminous, with light being rendered omnidirectional."[33]

33. Wesley, n.p.

Needless to say, no such perceptive criticism appeared at the time of the exhibition in Paris. The landscape designer Fletcher Steele reported favorably on both gardens to his American colleagues, who were mostly preoccupied with their application of historical motifs to decorate the country-house estates that were springing up from coast to coast. But for all its daring, Guevrékian's attempt to translate Cubist painting into a garden may have been too literal. The real elements of a garden—time, space, and the materials of earth, water, and plants—must be combined according to their own unique qualities. "A canvas of earth, flowers and water" as

Wesley concludes, it remained a static object for a spectator, falling short in landscape animation, nor was one invited to create tension and animation as one does in a space by Luis Barragán. The paradox of the Cubist garden was unresolved: how to transform the illusion of the space of a Cubist painting into actual three-dimensional garden art that must be experienced by the viewer at the horizontal level of the ground.

When the Exposition des Arts Décoratifs opened in Paris in 1925, the adventuresome and vivacious couple Charles and Marie-Laure de Noailles were preparing to hoist the red and yellow flag of the ancient Noailles family above their new winter villa on the Côte d'Azur. Designed by Mallet-Stevens, the villa was his first commissioned house. On a hill overlooking Hyères, the clean, bold volumes of the house seemed to settle well into the stone ruins of the medieval castle and ramparts. The worldly, spirited owners of Mallet-Stevens's villa entertained artists, commissioned avant-garde music, and conspired with new filmmakers—exemplifying the best of that extraordinary generation who lived on the cutting edge of change. The furnishings of Pierre Chareau, and the bare flower room by the painter Theo van Doesburg underlined the modernist viewpoint of the architect and of the de Noailles. The de Noailles' collection of paintings by Picasso, Braque, Gris, Chagall, Ernst, and Miró were brought out one at a time to be contemplated in Japanese fashion.

Mallet-Stevens had responded to the hilly terrain at Hyères as a fundamental element of his composition, leaving ample space for the Viscount's gardens. Of his generation, de Noailles was perhaps the only French amateur gardener equal to the Harold Nicolsons, Lawrence Johnston, and others in England but exhibited far more daring and imagination than his English contemporaries. When de Noailles saw Guevrékian's little triangle garden in Paris, he knew immediately where it would fit: into a wedge-shaped piece of ground at the new villa. He also knew exactly how he wanted Guevrékian's composition to incorporate a small bronze sculpture by Jacques Lipchitz called *Joie de Vivre* to be set on a small, motorized turning base.

Plan for Gabriel Guevrékian's garden design for the 1925 Exposition des Arts Décoratifs (Racine, Boursier-Mougenot, and Binet, *The Gardens of Provence and the French Riviera*, The MIT Press)

The villa and garden are now so dilapidated and altered that it is impossible to get an accurate sense of the place as it existed when it was completed. The surviving black and white photographs are unable to conjure the essential element of color in the composition, but Morton Shand's contemporary description in an essay called "A Villa of the Adroit," helps to recapture a garden that pushed garden design into the modern era:

The two sides of the equilateral triangle, of which this back wall forms the base are enclosed within symmetrical white-washed walls. These start flush with the top of the drawing room windows where they are pierced by twin doorways which open onto the lower road on one side and through the yard of the garage, the upper on the other and then drop down to the level of the heads of the tulips in the flower beds, to converge into the circumambulating symbolism of *Joie de Vivre*. Lipchitz's six-foot statue had been placed on a cylindrical drum enclosing a motor to rotate the work.

The awkward corners between these doorways and the back wall have been adroitly utilized to form tiers of miniature beds filled with rocky plants of two contrasting shades of green that zigzag up to the level of the lintels of the windows like climbing mountain roads seen from afar. This same saw-tooth design is repeated along the better part of the side walls in larger beds planted with masses of blue flowers. Directly in front of the drawing room windows are a couple of Chinese orange trees, each of which is set in the middle of a small herbed square of grass surrounded by white cement embedded with cubes of rather glassy black ceramic mosaic. Beyond this little parterre the chess-boarding rises in four almost imperceptible gradations of alternate planted and unplanted squares....The planted squares are filled with tulips, while the cemented ones are tasselated according to their respective gradations in unpatterned red, gray, blue, and yellow mosaic. Beyond the basin again and in line with the drawing-room door that opens onto the parterre, is a short pathway of violet

34. Quoted in
Wesley, n.p.

**mosaic leading to the pedestal drum of M. Lipchitz's rather untidy looking
masterpiece.**[34]

In 1926, Guevrékian designed another Cubist garden, at the Villa Heim, where the garden was
viewed mainly from a roof terrace, a distinctive twentieth-century innovation. In Le Corbusier's
"five points" of architecture—free plan, pilotis, free facade, horizontal strip window, and a roof
garden—only the space beneath the pilotis and the roof garden offered the garden designer
even a minimal opportunity to collaborate. The progress through the modern villa was no
longer to be on a horizontal Beaux Arts plane, extending out from the architecture, but was to
reach up vertically to the garden on the roof. For Corbusier, these self-contained spaces on
the roof high above the city were ideals beyond the existence of their practical realization.
They were to exist in a mysterious, animated state even when they were empty.

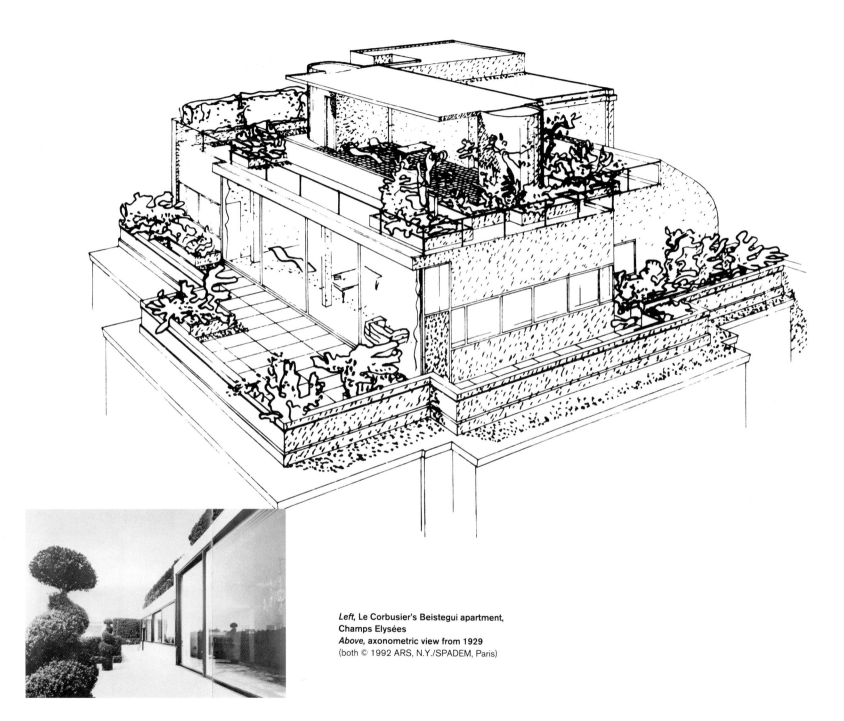

Left, Le Corbusier's Beistegui apartment,
Champs Elysées
Above, axonometric view from 1929
(both © 1992 ARS, N.Y./SPADEM, Paris)

1940. The Defeat! The Exodus! Paris is emptying. The roof-garden on the eighth floor remains alone.…The forsaken garden reacts, does not waste away: the wind, birds, and insects bring seeds. Some find a favorable environment.…Up there, the sun and wind reign over the garden. Plants and bushes orient and settle according to their needs. Once again nature reconquers its own rights. From now on the garden is abandoned to its fate."[35]

35. Quoted in Pierre-Alain Croset, "Roof Garden: The 'Technical Reason' and the Aesthetic Ideal," *Rassegna* (Bologna), no. 8 (October 1981), n.p.

In 1936, four years before he composed this reverie, Corbusier was invited to Brazil by a group of young architects exhilarated with the prospects of designing a high-rise building for the Ministry of Education and Health commissioned by the government that was to be located in the middle of downtown Rio de Janeiro. They had asked Corbusier to collaborate with them. The new government had, for the first time, agreed to commit itself to modern architecture in the latest international style. A roof garden was envisioned on the terrace roof of the ministry, and Roberto Burle Marx (born 1909), a young artist who had been working on a mural for the building, was asked to design it. This commission was the beginning of one of the most significant careers in garden design of the twentieth century. During the intervening fifty years, Burle Marx has produced a body of work without precedent in its range of diversity and originality. Ignoring the repeated calls for "unity" between architecture and its setting by critics and practitioners, he has managed to impose his own aesthetics produced by the often contrapuntal unity of art and nature that can complement, ignore, or simply overwhelm the architecture according to the artist's dictates.

Even though he is most celebrated internationally for his brilliant use of native tropical plants, Burle Marx was first attracted to their exotic possibilities not in the Amazon valley of Brazil but in the hothouses of the Dahlem Botanic Gardens in Berlin. He had gone to Germany with his parents in 1928–29 and had considered singing as a career before taking up painting. When he returned to Rio de Janeiro, he entered the National School of Art, where he became acquainted with an extraordinary group of teachers, architects, and designers. His first commission was for a roof terrace of a small house designed by Lúcio Costa and a talented young immigrant, Gregori Warchavchik. Warchavchik had introduced the ideals of functional architecture to Brazil in 1928 when his first modern house was completed in São Paulo, developing a style that was, in the words of Walter Gropius, "the inevitable logical product of the intellectual, social, and technical conditions of our age."[36] Through the purity of its geometric form and rhythmically balanced asymmetry, Warchavchik's work, and that of other Brazilians with whom Burle Marx was to collaborate, the spirit of modern architecture was planted in rich, tropical soil.

36. Gropius, p. 20.

Following the success of his gardens for the Ministry of Education, Burle Marx received many commissions and international recognition unusual for a landscape architect, or "landscape gardener" as he prefers to call himself. His garden for the villa he designed in 1948 for his friend Odete Monteiro was his first major work outside an urban environment. The nondescript Monteiro house was quite forgettable, so Burle Marx simply ignored it as he turned his attention to the spectacular mountainscape in the distance. Reaching out to this vast and forbidding reality, he would establish a man-made unity through his man-made, unnatural garden creation. The Monteiro garden was famous even before it had achieved maturity and was published only three years after it had been completed.

In 1956, speaking of the previous two decades of architectural efflorescence in Brazil, the critic and historian Sigfried Giedion asked how all this explosion was to be "related to nature in the environment in which it is taking place, with its tropical growth that one can almost feel bodily."[37] The answer was Burle Marx. He had mastered the art of transposing principles of painting into three dimensions on a horizontal plane, yet maintaining at the same time a coherent articulation of the garden's organization for the viewer as he moves through the work itself. Burle Marx has repeatedly said that a garden is not a painting with plants, even though the appealing graphics of his plans have misled even some of his admirers. Nor is it necessarily an inevitable extension of the architecture, as Joseph Olbrich and others had

37. Mindlin, Introduction, p. 6.

predicted earlier in the century. In the garden planned for Oscar Niemeyer's house commissioned in 1947 by Mr. and Mrs. Burton Tremaine, Burle Marx takes the lyrical refrain hinted at by the architecture and transforms it into a major concerto. While unity and harmony have been achieved, the "firm nucleus of the house" projected into the landscape by the regulating lines of the architecture that Olbrich called for, has been co-opted into a partnership by the countervailing force of the garden.

Burle Marx is also a scientific student of plants, understanding them and their personalities. He observes them for their color, texture, and growing habits in order to make plants do what building materials and structural elements do for architecture. There are the low-growing grasses that he has used for flat, checkered lawns; there are the ferns and bromeliads he weaves into vertical elements; and there are the giant floating platforms of red and green water lilies he uses to break up the open space of pools. His ability to manipulate this living material is a skill perfected over long years of research, allowing his art to take control of the raw material of nature. It has given him the power to negate the wildness of nature, removing its aura by its mutation into art. In the beginning Burle Marx's commissions were limited to fairly small projects where his horticultural bravura was thought to be his triumph and his limitation. But by the 1950s he was exploring the problems of urban regeneration on a scale that would eventually allow him to extend his visions over miles of reclaimed seafront in the heart of Rio at Flamengo Park and the Copacabana Beach. At an early stage of his development, Burle Marx was well aware of the advances of architecture over landscape design in the use of materials, of rational design based upon new techniques and in the determination of architects to make architecture address the issues of the modern world. The pronouncements of Le Corbusier and the dogma of the Bauhaus had reached the talented circle of architects studying and working in São Paulo and Rio de Janeiro. Many of them had traveled and studied in Europe. The Ecole National des Beaux-Arts, where Burle Marx studied, required painting students to study architecture, while architecture students were exposed to painting. In this it was similar to the Bauhaus, where the various arts of painting, architecture, theater, photography, and crafts were brought into an association that ignored the conventional distinctions. Yet professional architects worked chiefly with buildings, leaving the larger landscape to garden designers, which, of course, provided Burle Marx with the opportunity to work with talented contemporary architects who appreciated his work.

This synergetic cooperation among the arts advanced by the Bauhaus had circulated throughout Europe in the twenties. The Bauhaus saw the future of art and design as primarily involved with industry and mass production. Individual talent and skills were clearly to be subordinated to the social, economic, and spiritual needs of the larger society. Given the focus of Walter Gropius, founder of the Bauhaus, it was difficult to establish precisely how garden design and landscape architecture were to accommodate the "clear, organic architecture, whose inner logic will be radiant and naked, unencumbered by lying facades and trickeries," as he envisioned it.[38] An architecture with such high moral voltage seemed to require an Edenic setting of primordial purity. Hypnotized by this image, "the modern movement would not so much cultivate nature as they would cradle their buildings within it," in the words of Kenneth Frampton.[39] Throughout his career, Le Corbusier would often conjure a kind of unspoilt Virgilian landscape to embrace his austere temples and villas. His high-rise apartments, as he described them for his 1925 Plan Voisin, seem to occupy an ideal world levitating above a romantic, naive topography:

38. Bayer, Gropius, and Gropius, p. 27.

39. Frampton, p. 43.

On one side of the floors of the luxury houses—the new rue de la Paix, on the other side, green spaces extending far from the city. This is a sea of trees and here and there are the pure prismatic forms of majestic crystals, gigantic and limpid. Majesty, serenity, joy, sprightliness....Night has fallen. Like a crowd of meteors on a summer equinox, the cars trace trails of fire along the autoroute. Two hundred meters above on the roof gardens of the sky-scrapers are large paved terraces planted with spindle trees, bay trees, ivy, and embellished with tulips or geraniums set in parterres or crossed paths,

lined with a mixture of vivacious flowers....Other gardens far away on every side, at the same level seem like flat platforms of suspended gold.[40]

40. Bayer, Gropius, and Gropius, Preface.

The surrounding landscape of the famous Villa Savoie in the suburbs of Paris was to be the epitome of "Arcadian nature bathed in that benevolent, Classical light evoked by Poussin, replete with tall grass reaching up to the windows and cows resting in the middle distance."[41] Le Corbusier had conceived the villa itself as an abstract plan projected onto an imagined Cartesian grid. The pure form of the house confronts the countryside in all directions, recalling the idealized relationship Palladio had established between nature and his Villa Rotunda. The Villa Savoie manifests "the will of man isolated in the midst of irrational domains of freely growing vegetation."[42] Nature itself will not be violated but only contemplated at a distance through windows, openings, and terraces. While light and air will enter at all directions, nature will never merge with Le Corbusier's man-made machine. Whether on the roof of a high-rise or terrace of a suburban villa, Corbusier kept nature at arm's length. It was an Olympian remove to the intimate medium of gardens and landscape—plants, trees, water, earth—a panoramic vision that critics found of little use in trying to work out a coherent theory of design. Similarly, except in vaguely classical settings reminiscent of a drawing by Schinkel, Mies van der Rohe seems even less susceptible to or at ease with the power of nature. Throughout the thirties Mies's classical houses kept the landscape at bay, framed by glistening sealed windows or enclosed in an atrium. While Christopher Tunnard (1910–1979), the Canadian landscape architect working in England, clearly admired Mies van der Rohe's contemporary architectural vocabulary, the German master's work provided little ground in which to build a sympathetic garden. He is not even mentioned in Elizabeth Kassler's *Modern Gardens and the Landscape* (1964), published by the Museum of Modern Art in its first recognition of landscape architecture as a significant expression of contemporary design.

41. Ibid.

42. Ibid.

Tunnard wrote in his landmark *Gardens in the Modern Landscape,* "The modern garden architect has as much to discard as has the painter, sculptor and architect of a decade or two

43. Tunnard,
*Gardens in the
Modern Landscape,*
p.69.

44. Ibid.

45. Bayer, Gropius,
and Gropius,
Preface.

ago."[43] First published in 1938, this book was a valiant attempt to provoke a critical discussion of the theory of garden art beyond the prevailing academic fashions. Garden design was mired in a tradition that had, in his words, left the designer with "so many comforting, if worthless, technical aids of planning that very little could be left to guide him."[44] There remained, in his opening chapters on the evolution of landscape architecture, however, a taint of ambiguity regarding the uses of historical styles and precedents. Speaking of the English gardens of Switzer, Addison, Pope, and Bridgeman, Tunnard believed that in "their medley of styles" and the quality of transition and compromise that distinguished the early eighteenth century, they were closely related to contemporary conditions and the need to find a middle course. In his thoughtful appreciation of historical styles, however, Tunnard somehow lacked the dogmatic rigor that Gropius and Le Corbusier brought to their polemics when they urged architects and designers to take a central, vital role in the shaping of the twentieth century, without regard for history. As Alfred H. Barr, Jr., wrote in 1938, summing up the principles of the Bauhaus movement, "the student architect or designer should be offered no refuge in the past but should be equipped for the modern world."[45]

Tunnard recognized the tenacious hold English garden traditions imposed both on the profession and the gardening public. The English garden, like the Sunday English dinner, was the same throughout the land, someone remarked. His assessment that English gardens were the last bulwark of romanticism and sentimentality was square on the mark. But his guide "towards a new technique" seems to offer only more styles as alternatives. Any fundamental theory and criticism in the new sources of inspiration he identified—functionalism, Oriental garden aesthetics, and the abstractions of modern art—was oblique. Garden makers needed to take a lesson in functional planning from modern architects. Here he pointed to pragmatic, utilitarian gardens planned as a group effort by Swedish landscape architects imbued with the egalitarian ideals of the 1930s. In these modest efforts imbued with a humanistic, rational, collective spirit, perhaps a way to come to terms in the modern industrial world could be divined and exploited. Eastern aesthetics, and particularly Japanese art with its innate spiritual

The Villa Church, by Le Corbusier
(© 1992 ARS, N.Y./SPADEM, Paris)

qualities, had many parallels in contemporary Western aesthetics. Modern designers should study and cultivate these empathetic attitudes toward nature and the environment. As for modern art, Tunnard was even more vague as to the precise lessons it could teach contemporary garden designers. Instruction should begin, however, by critically evaluating and restricting decoration, ornament, and color in favor of modern systems and schemes. *Gardens in the Modern Landscape* did manage to bring into the discussion, for its English-speaking audience, a hint of the bracing criticism of leaders of the Modern movement on the Continent reaching back to Guevrékian, Adolf Loos, and Le Corbusier. A photograph of Guevrékian's triangular garden at Hyères is reproduced, and a detail of André Vera's garden at Saint-Germain-en-Laye is also included, with approval but with no analysis, leaving these experiments isolated and irrelevant.

While admiring the progressive architectural forms of Le Corbusier's work and quoting his attack on entrenched academic tradition as an inspiration for landscape architects, Tunnard expressed dismay at Corbusier's ideological retreat into the long grass of the Virgilian meadow at his villa at Poissy. It was a perceptive criticism that went to the heart of attitudes shared by many of the architects of the Modern movement. The foremost spokesman for the Modern movement had written:

I shall place this house on columns in a beautiful corner of the countryside. We shall have twenty houses rising above the long grass of a meadow where cattle will continue to graze. Instead of the superfluous and detestable clothing of garden city roads and byways, the effect of which is always to destroy the site, we shall establish a fine arterial system running in concrete through the grass itself, and in the open country. Grass will border the roads; nothing will be disturbed—neither the trees, the flowers nor the flocks and herds. The dwellers in these houses, drawn hence through love of the life of the countryside, will be able to see it maintained intact from their

hanging gardens or from their ample windows. Their domestic lives will be set in a Virgilian dream.[46]

46. Quoted in Tunnard, *Gardens in the Modern Landscape*, p. 78.

Or as Sigfried Giedion put it in an encomium to Richard Neutra: "The power to leave nature undisturbed and simultaneously to draw her into a specific emotional situation, reveals the artist no less than the power to transfuse a ferro-concrete skeleton with psychic value."

Tunnard saw that Le Corbusier had pursued the Romantic landscape philosophy to its logical conclusion but it was literally a dead end. "Few people," he pointed out, "want to be condemned to languish at a window and exercise exclusively on a roof garden."[47] It is a commentary on this laggard state of affairs that as late as the 1930s Tunnard's own garden designs in England would be considered pioneering. But his refusal to succumb to nature worship on the one hand and his contemporary sensibilities on the other did translate into some gardens of originality. He avoided the English predilection for improvisation, insisting that a garden was a work of art to be developed in a plan, a carefully worked out aesthetic composition, like a poem or a piece of music. His sensitive appreciation of the English eighteenth-century landscape garden was tempered by the fact that it was under irreversible siege by suburbia and industrialization throughout the English countryside. At St. Ann's Hill, an old Picturesque park left over from the eighteenth century and its collection of later horticultural exotica was restored and given a new lease as background for the new house designed by Raymond McGrath. Closer to the house, Tunnard was able to introduce a more intimate contemporary garden that was completely sympathetic with the unornamented, geometric architecture, demonstrating his design philosophy in a well-ordered, balanced relationship between the house and the landscape. Until the *ville contemporaine* and its new landscape became a reality, he concluded, "those eighteenth century landscapes which remain will suffice most of us and can be adapted to our needs."[48]

47. Ibid.

48. Ibid., p. 127

In the end, Tunnard confessed that he did not think that the private garden had much of a future. "The garden of tomorrow will not be the hedged, personal, half-acre of today," he wrote,

49. Ibid., p. 138

"but a unit of broad green landscape itself, controlled for the benefit of all."[49] Nature was not, as some contemporary architects thought, to be a refuge and escape from life but rather to serve "as an invigorator and a stimulus to body and mind."

In 1937, a year before Tunnard emigrated to the United States to teach at Harvard University where he was to meet an extraordinary generation of students ready to challenge the entrenched orthodoxy of the Olmsted school, the San Francisco Museum mounted an exhibition called "Contemporary Landscape Architecture." It was a singular event but too modest and isolated to generate much critical reaction or reorientation of garden design philosophy. Like England, the United States had been slow to respond to the changes that had already revolutionized painting, sculpture, and architecture, producing a second and even a third generation of international talent by the late 1930s. A chronic vision of natural, wide-open spaces kept many American landscape architects enthralled while others were caught up in an effort to bring American achievements into the mainstream of old, European culture by importing both ideas and artifacts for eager clients.

Following the First World War, a growing interest in early American art and architecture had begun to attract a new generation of students and admirers, especially in the South, whose fascination was not merely antiquarian or genealogical. Virginia, Maryland, and the Carolinas in particular took a belated interest in what had once been the most developed garden tradition in the former British colonies in the eighteenth and early nineteenth centuries. The interest stimulated by the restoration work at Williamsburg, Virginia, encouraged William Bottomley and other architects to turn to indigenous sources of inspiration for the new villas and gardens they were building for their rich, sophisticated clients, providing an alternative, native style grand enough to challenge imported Italian or English models. Handsome new books with elegant Beaux Arts elevations, drawings, and plans lifted James River plantation houses and Charleston town gardens to a level of cultivation that seemed equal to European examples of domestic architecture. In these old, often ruined gardens there was an element of romantic fantasy that appealed to Americans and their growing self-awareness of a maturing nation.

Lacking any recognized garden tradition of its own, California turned to Europe, as most Easterners had been doing for a very long time and with more confidence since Edith Wharton

William Lawrence Bottomley's plan for
Milburne, 1934

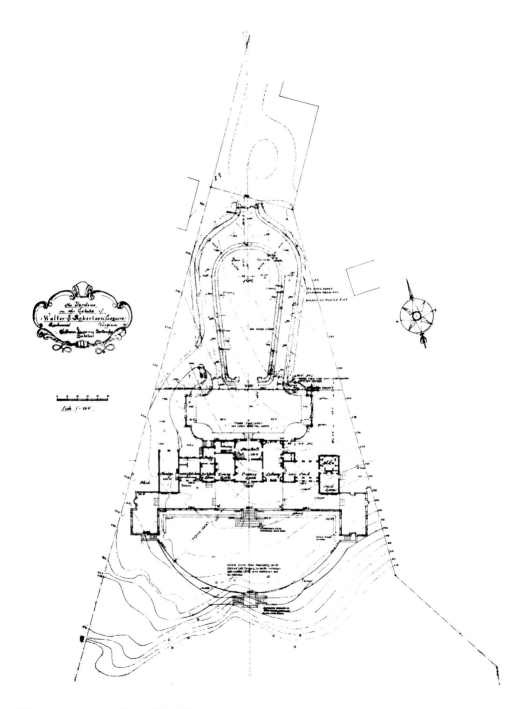

Grounds for Change

had admonished them on correct garden taste. The vast horticultural possibilities of California and its new, aggressive wealth inspired highly catholic and liberal borrowings from Europe that in fact violated most of Wharton's rules. "Overnight palaces and villas seem to spring into being on barren hills and wooded canyons," Winifred Starr Dobyns gushed in 1931.[50] "Within a year a garden will blossom where yesterday greenwood and scrub clothed the ground." She no doubt had in mind Harold Lloyd's Beverly Hills extravaganza created for the movie star in the Benedict Canyon by A. E. Hanson. Hanson was a California high school drop-out who had worked for Silver Screen garden design in the early 1920s. Within a decade he had created throughout Southern California literally scores of posh, expensive gardens instantly realized and as photogenic as movie sets. The Hollywood speed and glamour would become the model for even grander instant creations at the casino hotels like the Mirage in Las Vegas by the end of the century.

50. Quoted in Gebhard and Lynds, p. 15.

Yet by the 1930s, largely through the work of Thomas Church (1902–1978), a few young Californians had begun to reject the make-believe, *retardataire* values Hanson's work represented. They were not confused in the way Norman T. Newton seemed to be in 1932 when he wrote:

The conscious effort to "go modern" by creating dizzy patterns and weird plant forms which may appear beautiful to some observers, and the use of a pretentious symbolism to which some have referred as a source of emotion, may yet have an undiscovered appeal to the senses rather than to the thought-process, but at best they seem to be purely extraneous intellectual exercises. We must direct our efforts toward a more nearly complete understanding of the essentials of our design, to the function and purpose of things, to the beauty latent in them, and to the merits of the results. The landscape architect must devote his energies to the application of changeless principles to our mode of living; the question of "modern" or "not modern" will take care of itself.[51]

51. Newton, p. 303.

Thomas Church studied at the University of California, Berkeley, and at Harvard in the late 1920s. The tradition of the Beaux Arts was still the established faith when Church arrived in Cambridge. This heritage was somewhat mitigated by education reforms initiated in 1928 by the American Society of Landscape Architects, when it adopted a "Statement of Minimum Educational Requirements in Landscape Architecture." But beginning courses were still renderings of classical terraces and courtyard gardens ending with settings for colonial gymnasiums and Romanesque skyscrapers. The year of the exhibition in San Francisco, Church had made his second visit to Europe where he met the Finnish designer and architect Alvar Aalto. Aalto's organic, curvilinear forms were drawn from his mystical reverence for nature rooted in his inherited native Scandinavian pragmatism. This vernacular source of contemporary inspirations for Aalto's functional, clean, aesthetic values immediately impressed the susceptible Californian. Church's entry in the San Francisco exhibition was for a small residential plot twenty-five feet wide, in which he exuberantly linked the interior space of the house with the outside, ignoring all historical props or rules in its clear-cut lines, anticipating his sympathy for Aalto's work, which he would soon discover.

In his reliance on nature as a model and his "biological" philosophy of life, Aalto has rejected the frayed paradigms of European garden traditions, yet expressed at the same time a skepticism of Le Corbusier's social visions of people communing with nature from the rooftops of skyscrapers while living like ants in their engineered world. Aalto's affinity for the organic forms of nature and for natural topography can be seen in Church's hilltop setting for his famous El Novillero garden at Sonoma, California, begun in 1947. The rocky hillsides, the salt marshes, and the heavy woods are all reinterpreted in Church's abstract, elegant composition conceived through the prism of Cubist aesthetics.

Aalto, like Tunnard and other designers of the 1930s, was increasingly fascinated with the aesthetics of Japanese culture and art built on a profound understanding of nature. What was it exactly that gave Japanese gardens a more structural solidity and depth than most gardens

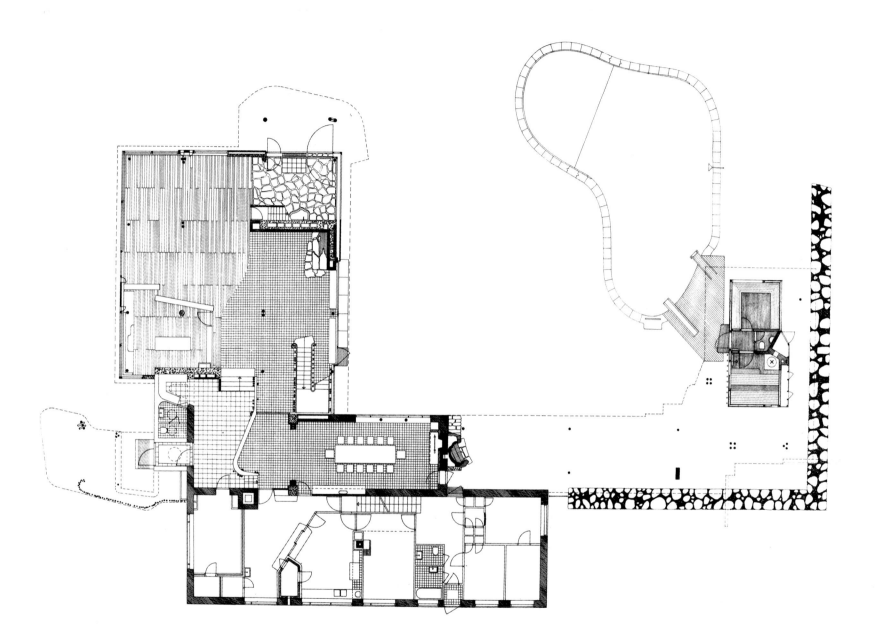

Plan of Villa Mairea, with paved wintergarden
(Courtesy Alvar Aalto Foundation)

in the West, whose "gardens…by comparison seem frail, shallow, insubstantial, and meaningless?"[52]

52. Engel, p. 16.

The Japanese economy in handling of line, form, and materials in small garden spaces seemed to have a particular relevance for contemporary garden design issued in the increasingly urbanized West. In 1935 Aalto paid romantic tribute to "Japanese culture which, with its limited range of raw materials and forms, has implanted in the people virtuosity in creating variation and new combinations almost daily."[53] One hardly needs to be reminded how far industrialized Japan of the late twentieth century has departed from Aalto's idealized image of the people's "virtuosity" he had known only in books and from discussions with Japanese friends in Finland.

53. Schildt, p. 113.

Even if the Great Depression hadn't delivered the final blow, Thomas Church recognized that the era of the grand, often vulgar estate garden in America was coming to an end, aesthetically, culturally, and economically. The philosophy of the Beaux Arts or of the warmed-over Olmstedian principles of city planning had nothing to offer the ubiquitous American backyard or the out-of-door life of California or Florida. Landscape architects, it was thought, should be giving more professional attention to the small residential garden and to the possibilities of communal gardens, which had been opposed by many, as Tunnard pointed out, owing to a misplaced fear of loss of individual liberty even though middle-class freedom of choice had been severely circumscribed by economic forces far beyond its control or influence. For some, the very idea of a shared community garden sounded like the radical environmental and social critique first offered by the Socialist Peter Kropotkin in his *Factory, Fields and Workshops,* published in 1896.

In 1924 Fletcher Steele addressed the issues of the small suburban garden in a how-to manual, *Design for the Small Garden*. Its informal, down-to-earth tone was startling and some thought it undignified for a professional landscape architect to be willing to reveal professional secrets to an ignorant public. Yet Steele recognized that the ubiquitous American yard was a unique cultural statement that deserved at least minimal professional criticism. Collectively, it was far more important in its critical mass and messiness than all the professionally designed gardens could ever aspire to be. While offering a practical guide for the amateur house owner of average means, he also included an overdue criticism of the American middle-class prejudice against privacy, an attitude that had produced the American lawn—"indeterminate areas covered with grass like a few fishballs on a large platter."[54] Placing the house on a 50 by 75 by 100-foot lot left it strangely isolated in the middle of its monotonous front lawn—a procedure that was repeated with every lot down the street. "Tradition says practically that it makes no difference what is done on a place if only there be an open front lawn on the street side.…But our work and thought should go to improving and maintaining those parts of our grounds in which we can live in privacy and comfort."[55] Recent critics have maintained that Steele's book prophesied "the age of Functionalism…years before Stein and Wright showed their Radurn scheme" by advocating the reversal in housing of the common practice of living-room-facing-the-street, kitchen-facing-the-rear of the property. Steele recognized the change in the lifestyle from homecraft self-dependence to an intermediate, mass-production economy.[56] Steele also pin-pointed America's cultural impoverishment in its chronic failure to develop an indigenous garden life on the order of the French or Italians. "The man who will wrestle with his architect over a wasted foot of bedroom will never stop to think about a larger area wasted out of doors. And in the wasting he will go without what would furnish him with much pleasure—a garden within which to sit and read and see his friends as in Paris and in Rome."[57]

In his introduction to the San Francisco Museum catalogue *Contemporary Landscape Architecture*, Henry-Russell Hitchcock expressed the thought that terraces and outdoor living rooms offered the "chief possibilities for formal gardening which is in keeping with the character of modern architecture"[58] and, he might have added, with the values of his California audience. As for a theory of modern gardening in all of its manifestations, he pronounced that the general rule and guide must be "the preservation of all possible values previously in

54. Steele, *Design for the Small Garden*, p. 25.

55. Ibid., p. 12.

56. Karson, p. 68.

57. Steele, *Design for the Small Garden*, p. 13.

58. *Contemporary Landscape Architecture*, n.p.

existence in the landscape setting." Man-made intervention must be held to an absolute minimum. Nature's pristine benevolence is to be protected and embraced. The dictum of "less is more" was to be applied to the landscape as well as to the architecture. Hitchcock recognized that such a theory severely limited the possibilities of art and creative garden making for the individual house. But the ramifications of these limitations "brings within the field of gardening at the other end of the scale whole fields of regional and even national planning as well as important aspects of urbanism…"[59] It would, he claimed, restore gardening's share of aesthetic attention, which it had once enjoyed as an important part of civilization in the Baroque and Romantic age.

In 1936, a young student from California met Fletcher Steele at Harvard, where Steele was lecturing. Garrett Eckbo (1910–) was deeply impressed by Steele's openness to the new ideas then transforming painting, sculpture, and architecture. Steele's worldly, sophisticated personality, which was reflected in his perfectionist and expensive creations, was also hard for either student or client to resist. Steele had seen the 1925 Paris Exposition des Arts Décoratifs and was enthusiastic about the concrete "trees" that had been created for Mallet-Stevens's exhibition garden. Steele's critical attitude, demonstrated by his questioning of professional and historical assumptions, more than his designs, appealed to Eckbo, who had joined with James Rose and Dan Kiley to begin their own student debates on the future of landscape design.[60] The energetic arguments that they introduced into their discussions, brought together in three parts for *Architectural Record* in 1939–40, helped to shift the emphasis farther away from the conventional preoccupations with the private garden, as Hitchcock had predicted. Eckbo's own recollection of the years that marked a turning point in landscape design is an essential document of modern landscape history:

When I arrived at Harvard in 1936 as a green Californian from the frontier, I encountered a school in which the landscape faculty felt that since trees were not made in factories, it was not necessary for the profession to concern itself with new

59. Ibid.

60. Karson, p. 232.

ideas in architecture or the arts. The old tried-and-true formal/informal system had worked since the eighteenth century and would continue to be comfortable and reliable.

Inasmuch as we were downstairs in Robinson Hall and architecture was upstairs, it was difficult for us to avoid what was going on up there. Dean Joseph Hudnut had arrived a few years before, determined to modernize architecture. In 1937, he brought Walter Gropius from England. The atmosphere of the Graduate School of Design was charged, controversial and exciting. Of the twenty students in landscape architecture, three—Dan Kiley, Jim Rose and I—were so turned on by the new ideas upstairs that on our own we began to explore new forms and arrangements which might reflect the new design ideas. In our experience at Harvard, we did learn about earlier efforts in Europe, particularly Christopher Tunnard in England and Pierre le Grand in France.

At the same time, in San Francisco, unbeknownst to us, Thomas Church, influenced by William Wurster and other modernist architects, began a similar exploration in his garden practice. The results of these two parallel efforts…became the modern design approach that has dominated American landscape architecture through the middle of the century. Basically it made it possible to eliminate preconceived design vocabularies, and to develop forms and arrangements which spoke to specific sites, clients, local contexts and regional cultures.[61]

61. Garrett Eckbo.

Dan Kiley recalls how he and Eckbo and Rose considered themselves "outcasts," enjoying each other's stimulating company more than "boring lectures and an ideology that nipped the past.…One thing that set everybody back was that the History of Landscape Architecture course was so dull and so bad that we just hated anything to do with the past. In some ways that happened to be good, when Gropius had just come in, cutting off the past right like that."[62] In spite of his youthful rebellion, Kiley's mature work expresses a sense of historical

62. Byrd, Jr. and Rainey, p. 24.

rootedness and continuity that must be linked with the discipline he received from his Beaux Arts teachers at Harvard. The formal riverfront promenade he designed for Saarinen's Arch in St. Louis, his rows of native Virginia cedars marshaled in front of Saarinen's Dulles Airport, and the geometric groves of honey locusts and rows of magnolias set in rectangular planting beds at the Kennedy Library, in Dorchester, Massachusetts, are impressive contemporary interpretations of Beaux Arts principles. It is that quality that immediately distinguishes Kiley's work from that of his contemporaries Eckbo and Rose.

It is clear that there were surging changes in the air in the midthirties; fresh, experimental attitudes regarding art, life, and gardens that were by no means limited to Cambridge, Massachusetts, or Berkeley, California. There was also a feeling of foreboding as well as of anticipation. The same year that Roberto Burle Marx was working on his first garden commission with international implications—the roof garden for Le Corbusier's Ministry of Education and Health in Rio de Janeiro—there were those in Europe who thought the garden, like the novel, was finished. In 1937, Achille Duchêne, who had recently carried his elegant, classic garden reconstructions perfected in the Ile de France to the grounds of Blenheim Palace in Oxfordshire, England, where he designed noble water parterres for the Duke of Marlborough, flatly pronounced the art of the garden to be dead. He also published plans to illustrate the direction he thought the future might take. "They are gardens for use by the community," he wrote in *Les Jardins de l'Avenir*; "for education, and rest; gardens for sport, games and the enjoyment of all."[63]

63. Quoted in Jellicoe et al., p. 147.

Both Eckbo and James Rose at first concentrated on small domestic gardens in America. But Eckbo confessed that "residential design is the most intricate, specialized, demanding, responsible and frustrating field for the designer."[64] Later, moving away from Church and Rose in his interest in a wider environmental practice, Eckbo would take landscape design into the larger environment where city planners and developers were already staking out their avaricious claims. In 1949 he argued for a more responsible use of land, echoing Tunnard's

64. Ibid., p. 152.

position of more than ten years earlier. "The contradiction between social relations and individual land use, which exists in all our communities, is not between subdivision itself for unreasonable profit and land-use needs. The admission by all parties concerned, including most members of the banker-builder-realtor trinity, that earlier subdivision practices have been irresponsible, is in itself an admission of this contradiction."[65] Even though tragically little progress has followed from Eckbo's rational, critical argument for a more responsible public use of land, he identified the issues and provided a few models. His most significant public work was his proposed migrant worker camp in Texas, designed for the Farm Security Administration, and the Mar Vista subdivision in West Los Angeles. Both projects, although abstract and sculptural in plan, incorporated his belief in communal gardens planned for a variety of unpredictable needs.

65. Eckbo,
*Landscape for
Living*, p. 245.

66. Engel, p. 130.

Long before Rose discovered the Japanese and particularly the Zen traditions of garden making—"the abode of the unsymmetrical"—the gardens of Japan became well known in the United States and in Europe.[66] As early as 1886, Edward S. Morse, director of the Peabody Academy of Science, wrote a scholarly monograph called *Japanese Homes and Their Surroundings*. Japanese art was being collected in Paris and in Boston while Japanese literature and philosophy was beginning to appear in translation. Painters like Monet and van Gogh were as stimulated by Japanese prints as a later generation would be by African sculpture. When still a student, Frank Lloyd Wright avidly collected Japanese woodcuts. No international fair or trade exhibition was complete without a Japanese temple or teahouse. Things Japanese were as exotic and stimulating as African art would be a few decades later.

What was not easily understood either by Western garden designers or amateur gardeners, however, was the differences in climate between the steady, unvarying growing conditions of Japan and those of Europe or America. The rather static pattern of Japan's climate was far different from the dynamically changing seasons in the temperate zones of Surrey, England, or Connecticut. This was something that was difficult to convey in a book or a plant list. It was even more difficult to explain how the weather of Japan paralleled if not shaped the long Eastern views of the world, of life, and of Buddhist and Zen gardens. In practical terms this meant a subtle yet radical horticultural difference in the composition of a Japanese garden, where, for example, the wide use of frost-sensitive broadleaf evergreens dominates the garden's structure. This issue of precise, even profound horticultural knowledge and skills cultivated by Japanese gardeners for centuries was particularly daunting for American professionals who have no such background or heritage. The ability to convincingly adapt Japanese horticulture and its requirements of high maintenance to a foreign setting using technological shortcuts has been exceedingly hard to achieve. Tunnard, who was an accomplished plantsman, having studied at the Royal Horticultural Society's Wisley gardens, deplored the sentimental and superficial temptations of Oriental garden art to which so many had fallen prey.

Japanese garden design, even when it is imperfectly understood, has had a continuing influence on American and particularly Californian gardens since the first permanent model was constructed in 1894 at the California Midwinter Exposition in San Francisco. The Japanese Tea Garden designed and built by Makoto Hagiwara (1854–1925) in California was not a replica, as had been the exhibition garden sponsored by the Japanese government on the unpromising shores of Lake Michigan for Chicago's Columbian Exposition the year before. But the Ho-o-den temple in Chicago had not been without influence, having been seen by the susceptible young architect Frank Lloyd Wright. Hagiwara designed his garden for the site at Golden Gate Park with the traditional skills of all Japanese master gardeners. Hagiwara's reputation grew with a major commission to design another garden in 1906 for Eugen de Sabla at his ranch in California, known as El Cerrito. Hagiwara was able to take advantage of existing mature oaks, laurels, and specimen evergreens, giving the garden an immediate patina of age. Called The Garden Worthy of a Day of Contemplation, for many years it represented the finest interpretation of Japanese gardening in North America.

67. Brown, *European and Japanese Gardens*, Introduction.

In 1900, in order to popularize the recent discovery among American architects that "the garden should be designed in connection with the house,"[67] the American Institute of Architects made gardens one of the principal topics at its annual meeting. The organizers of the meeting listed the subjects presented in a hierarchy of their recognized importance—Italian gardens, English, then French—followed by a paper on Japanese gardens. The proceedings closed with "A Japanese Garden in California," a lecture by C. H. Townsend, illustrating Hagiwara's garden in the Golden Gate Park, in which the modest architecture of the teahouse was subordinated to the garden's composition. Noting that most people viewed the garden as a novelty, Townsend nevertheless sensed that it embodied an important lesson, even though he was vague about its particular message and application.

There was nothing vague in Frank Lloyd Wright's understanding of the unity between nature, architecture, and its material. Organically embedded in their natural surroundings and opening out to them with terraces, balconies, and cantilevered roofs, Wright's houses openly acknowledge their debt to Japanese sources. Whatever the vestiges of established axial principles that might be hidden in the surrounding foliage, Wright understood the unity between nature and form in Japanese art when he translated the Japanese interpenetration of indoor and outdoor space into his revolutionary American house. He was masterful in disguising the line between the earth and the architecture. The paving stones of walks and terraces are flush with doorsills, as Alexander Purves has pointed out in carefully observed details: "Glass is set directly into stone, and the glass is startlingly clear, having been fired three times. The corner mullion is eliminated where the glass is fixed and mitered, and at the casements it disappears completely when the windows are open. Interior planters obscure the

68. Purvis, p. 178.

sills of the window, so that indoor flowers join visually with the foliage outside."[68] In the plan of the Martin House, at Buffalo, New York (1904), the interlocking structures and their rooms form a spreading pattern, recalling the temple and garden complex of Byodo-in, dating from the Heian period of the eleventh century. Like the Martin House, this celebrated temple anticipated a certain Beaux Arts order through a series of formal axes strongly contrasting with its informal garden layout and differing radically with the much later stroll garden and imperial villa of Katsura outside Kyoto. Wright also used the device of low brick walls and vine-covered pergolas much as Japanese walks are used to tie the architecture to the site. Controlled greenery was also introduced by Wright into his planting spaces next to the walls to further unify the house and garden.

Both Rudolf Schindler (1887–1953) and Richard Neutra (1892–1970) shared Wright's sensitivity to the natural landscape and worked as his assistants in California. They would later explore the relationship between building and site in Wrightian terms. In 1927, for example, after Neutra finished the plans for his Health House in Los Angeles (a name that reflects his religious interest in what he called the "biological fitness" of design), the architect left for his first trip to Japan. His immediate response to the natural simplicity of Japanese design and its essential unity with its surroundings was somehow innate. For this young European architect recently transplanted to California, Japanese architecture conveyed its message in a universal language that could be grasped even by someone who had grown up in the crowded tenement blocks of Vienna at the turn of the century. It was an aesthetic kinship that both Wright before him, and Alvar Aalto later, were drawn to. The sensitive and rational way the vernacular Japanese house interacted with its surroundings was a revelation and inspiration. One of Aalto's secondhand sources of Japanese architecture was in fact a book written on the subject in 1927 by the German architect Bruno Taut. It was Taut who had discovered in Japan a prototype of the kind of architectural philosophy that he and other architects had been advocating even before the Bauhaus was established in 1919. Through Taut's efforts in Japan, the seventeenth-century Katsura Imperial Villa and gardens outside Kyoto were first brought to international attention and made an icon and symbol of Modernism. Later, Gropius would also appropriate Katsura's minimal refinements through carefully edited photographic details as a point of departure for modern design doctrine even though the villa and its extraordinary stroll garden had been produced by a feudal past that had nothing whatsoever to do with twentieth-century aesthetic values.

Richard Neutra never wrote much about garden design, but his *Mystery and Realities of the Site* and his memoirs, *Life and Shape*, in which a number of early landscape drawings are reproduced, provide a useful background to the intelligent and responsive landscape settings he created for his houses in the thirties and forties. His ideals are summed up in what he called his "search for elemental environmental factors…to which a human organism already has an adaptation of long standing, and to fit them into our design, applying in all this the insight of the biologist."[69] Neutra had actually apprenticed with the Swiss gardener Gustav Ammann in 1919, acquiring a certain familiarity with horticulture and site planning. Later, in Berlin, he carried out garden designs for the architects Erich Mendelsohn, Ernst Freud, and Arthur Korn. When he joined Rudolf Schindler in 1926, after moving to Los Angeles, his first work was to prepare garden plans for Schindler's Howe House in Los Angeles (1925) and the Lovell House at Newport Beach (1926). Neutra's first completely integrated house and site was

69. Neutra, *Life and Shape*, p. 329.

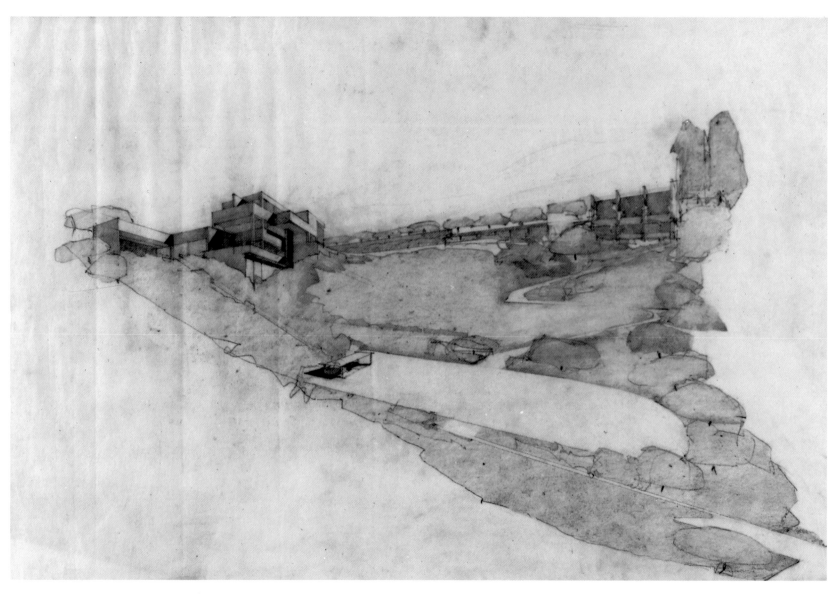

**An early design (1927) by Richard Neutra for
his Lovell House in Los Angeles**
(Richard Neutra Archive, Department of Special
Collections, UCLA Research Library)

his Health House, commissioned by a Los Angeles doctor who in 1927 accepted Neutra's vision of a "strange wide-open filigree steel frame, set deftly and precisely by cranes and booms onto this inclined piece of rugged nature…marrying it through view, air and radiation."[70]

70. Ibid., p. 221.

The Kaufmann Desert House, Neutra's masterpiece completed in 1947, sums up the twenty years of design advances Neutra was to continue to make following his early experiments in Los Angeles. By removing the walls of the living area, he was able to articulate "the linkage with the landscape," an idea he had tested earlier at the Health House, drawing "again on what the vitally dynamic natural scene had been for a hundred thousand years," to make it "once more…a human habitat." In the Kaufmann house, Neutra extended the cool, sleek living space and pool into the bare, rocky desert framed by distant hills, now scaled for human intimacy through its elegant appropriation of the architecture. The horizontal lines of the stark setting of the desert are emphasized by the clean surface of the wooden floor and the ceiling that hovers above the low planter boxes and table supporting a bonzai tree. There is, in its spare serenity, an affirmative statement that documents Neutra's successful search for a "biologically bearable" environment as a means of survival by design. "What is tolerable to nerves and what possesses form and pattern are indeed positive determinants."[71]

71. Ibid., p. 223.

"Any architecture that does not express serenity is a mistake," the landscape architect Luis Barragán declared, decrying the "intemperate use of enormous glass windows" in contemporary houses. Neutra's "generous opening to health agents" must have had the ring of a municipal sanitation commissioner to the sensuously cultivated imagination of the Mexican. Barragán saw a house and its garden as a refuge, an ancient tradition of walled privacy that ran from Mexico to Islamic Spain of the twelfth century and on into the garden mythology of the Middle East. Like Wright's recollections of growing up on a Wisconsin farm, Barragán's childhood memories of a rustic family life on a ranch near the village of Mazamitla remained a source of inspiration throughout his life. An element of nostalgia and memoir are never far below the surface of his work.

An engineer by training, Barragán had discovered the writings of Ferdinand Bac during his studies in Mexico, before meeting Bac in Europe. Bac's belief in "an art which builds upon all our nostalgic reminiscences of places where we would like to have set up our tent and remain, uplifted by Beauty and strengthened by Simplicity"[72] struck an emotional chord in Barragán. Bac's daring use of color in his neo-Mediterranean gardens along the French Riviera may have also influenced Barragán's own startling palette of pinks, yellows, and magentas to animate his austere architecture. Color used on wall planes is a key element in the austere composition of his gardens and houses, as are the sober but monumental forms. Paint is applied to the architectural garden elements like a stage set, giving his work a sense of theater, as Emilio Ambasz has observed, a property that the Modern movement has neglected or ignored altogether.[73] Barragán's use of color is also derived from the abstract color field proposed by contemporary artists.

72. Quoted in Racine, p. 112.

73. Ambasz, p. 106.

The Mexican came late to landscape architecture and his garden language is that of a poet retelling a myth in inexhaustible variations. His most complex creation (and the only project that is still maintained in its original condition) is the estate of San Cristobal, in the suburbs of Mexico City. The complex consists of a house, swimming pool, horse pool, and stable where thoroughbreds are raised and trained. The center of action is the stable, near the house, and the horses that live and are groomed there occupy a surreal theater set. Not since the great horse water tank at Marly was built in the late seventeenth century to terminate the water displays at Louis XIV's retreat have equine ablutions been elevated to such high art. In the house with its plaza, the trough projection feeding water into the horse pool, and in the paddock where grooms are choreographed to care for their charges, the analogue of Barragán's childhood village is made manifest in the ritual of his stunning creation.

It was a *pueblo* with hills, formed by houses with tile roofs and immense eaves to shield passersby from the heavy rains in the area. Even the earth color was interesting because it was red earth. In this village, the water distribution system consisted of great gutted logs, in the form of troughs, which ran on a support structure of tree forks, 5 meters above the roofs. This aqueduct crossed over the town, reaching the patios, where there were great stone fountains to receive the water. The patios housed the stables, with cows and chickens, all together. Outside, in the street, there were iron rings to tie the horses. The channeled logs, covered with moss, dripped water all over town, of course. It gave this village the ambiance of a fairy tale.[74]

74. Ibid., p. 9.

Throughout much of the century, self-doubt has regularly assailed landscape architects, adding to the growing confusion of belief and direction. Any reasoned idea for the focus of landscape architecture, its purpose, meaning, and methodology, continues to elude those who diligently question and search. The generalities and abstractions that afflict garden journalism have failed to move the debate in any meaningful way. In his book *Modern Gardens*, published in 1955, Peter Shepheard intended to identify "masterworks of international architecture" but confessed that examples were hard to find. "No large body of recognizably modern landscape architecture exists," he concluded.[75] All tradition of design was dead, and the time-honored system of apprenticeship had disappeared. The enemies of promise were myriad and it was hard to assess the extent of their debilitating influence. The failure to produce a modern movement in landscape design, Shepheard concluded, resulted from the absence of professional opportunities for avant-garde experiments, particularly in England. It was a condition that may also have grown out of the conflict between the traditional conservative techniques and materials of garden making and the revolutionary technical forces combined with the radical new materials that had transformed modern architecture.

75. Shepheard, Introduction, p. 13.

Ian McHarg's *Design with Nature* has provided recent generations of landscape architects and city planners with stirring moral dicta on the environment, but the writer was not able to indicate what form the landscape of his purified environment should look like or to point in a plausible direction. Garrett Eckbo and Dame Sylvia Crowe have laid out useful guidelines of responsible techniques to hone the designer's skills to react to or mirror outside influences. According to Crowe "the unchangeable laws of good proportion" in their "infinite variation" will supply the "serenity" by which all gardens should be judged.[76] No wonder there is despair in professional circles regarding the future of their calling.

76. Sylvia Crowe, *Garden Design* (West Sussex, England: Packard Press Limited, 1981), Introduction, pp. 10–12.

Grasping at labels such as "post-Modern" has encouraged a liberal use of contrived historical references in self-conscious garden designs as a kind of mask or decoration but with little relevance to the modern technological world. The publicity that post-Modern architecture has received has no doubt led some garden designers to emulate the same shallow concoctions. The easy-to-read narratives invoked by obvious references to the past or to misunderstood myths do have a certain journalistic appeal that encourages superficial commentary without real criticism. The same observations apply to the field of architecture, where post-Modern conceits cover up the aesthetic bankruptcy beneath the broken pediments, classical columns, and banal references to historical models of a distant and misunderstood past.

On the other hand, metaphor and analogy drawn from one's personal history and experience, as Barragán's has done, or borrowed from biology, ecology, or literature, have been used over the ages in defining the landscape. In his essay on landscape as theater, J. B. Jackson has argued that we need to explore a number of different metaphors drawn from human experience, just as painters and sculptors did at the beginning of this century. This is quite different from merely striving for effect or attention, as a number of contemporary designers have done. In a series of lectures in 1980–82, Sir Geoffrey Jellicoe offered his own idiosyncratic analysis of the design process to find out how landscape design could respond to the still unimaginable world revealed by Einstein, Picasso, and the American philosopher John Dewey. Dewey's provocative inclusion was justified by Sir Geoffrey because of the philosopher's theory that art was a continuum of the creative process itself rather than the completed discreet work. Garrett Eckbo also expressed his debt to Dewey when he declared that "design is a problem-solving activity," dismissing the historical precedence of design in the landscape as an irrelevant "history of special elements for special people."

Jellicoe gives the mind, and particularly the subconscious, primacy over the eye, analyzing a number of his own garden projects to identify, in retrospect, the sources of inspiration drawn from his own psyche. One of the obvious problems with this subjective, atavistic approach is attempting to account for the role of the client and his tastes and whims, an influence outside the artist's personality and psyche. Most of Jellicoe's examples are new gardens that have been inserted into old established landscapes where his English subconscious is free to play with the stimulus of English history. But in his recently created garden on the grounds of sixteenth-century Sutton Place, near Guildford, along a passage he has called "Homage" to the Surrealist painter Magritte, Jellicoe explains that the "purpose is to disorganize the mind by…the juxtaposition of disparate objects." Yet his use of monumental urns actually bought on impulse by the owner and placed by Jellicoe in front of a Tudor brick wall is quite conventional and seems to have nothing to do with Sir Geoffrey's psyche, let alone its Tudor surroundings.[77]

77. Sir Geoffrey Jellicoe, *The Guelph Lectures on Landscape Design*, p. 168.

Jellicoe's *Guelph Lectures* do not offer a foundation for the critical appraisal of historical or contemporary designs or even an argument that such critical appraisal might be an essential ingredient that is missing from discussions on landscape architecture. This seems to leave the field, as Steven Krog has pointed out, doubly cursed. "First in the absence of a critical mechanism for confronting the past, a progressive future remains elusive."[78] In turn, this condition has left the landscape architect vulnerable to irrelevant but tempting styles, particularly those of recent vintage such as neo-Modernism, that seduce in their appealing simplicity without ever coming to terms with the underlying historical issues.

78. Krog, "Whither the Garden," p. 102.

Christopher Tunnard's *Gardens in the Modern Landscape*, first appearing in the second quarter of the century, is about as close as we come to a survey of the threads of development that have shaped modern garden design but it falls far short of similar studies in other fields of the arts. There is, for example, nothing comparable to Nikolaus Pevsner's *The Sources of Modern Architecture and Design* or his *Pioneers of Modern Design*. This lack of a critical perspective on the recent past, in spite of some excellent monographs on individual artists, says something about the persistent failure of professional self-confidence.

Even though he speaks as a geographer and views the landscape in broad terms of the study of the earth and its life, J. B. Jackson suggests that despair may be premature. Jackson takes the long view, and it is perhaps too early to attempt any full understanding of those man-made creations that have been the subject of this essay. At best, he advises, we should rely most intently not on the technicians and planners, but rather on artists, philosophers and, of course, geographers. "They are the most trustworthy custodians of human traditions; for they seek to discover order within randomness, beauty within chaos, and the enduring aspirations of mankind behind blunders and failures."[79]

79. J. B. Jackson, *The Necessity for Ruins and Other Topics,* p. 75.

I am intrigued with the evocative possibilities hinted at by Jackson and especially by the inclusion of geographers as "trustworthy custodians of human traditions." Critics such as Jackson who have been willing to look closely at the American landscape with its parking lots, television aerials and satellite dishes, electrical substations, and fuel storage farms with their rows of glistening tanks, can indeed instruct and reveal a world that terrifies most garden designers along with a blindered public who want to escape from the realities of those necessary functions on which their lives and their values depend. But "the visible influence of technology is ubiquitous and nearly inescapable," Robert L. Thayer, Jr., has written, "even though we are made uncomfortable and often" alienated by its sinister presence.[80]

80. Thayer, p. 1.

Throughout the inquiry that has prompted this book, I have been struck by the refusal of the contemporary landscape architect to confront the "Machine in the Garden," as Leo Marx titled his landmark study.[81] In his investigation of the dilemma of modern technology, Marx called for "new symbols of possibilities" that might evolve out of our late-twentieth-century technologies. The issue of technology versus the landscape is truly profound, as Thayer has also eloquently argued. Thayer uses the example of the benign new sources of energy generated in vast wind farms where thousands of wind turbines have been planted across the foothills of central California. Anyone who has seen one of the awesome installations following the contours of the rolling land and electronically adjusting to the prevailing wind currents like a sunflower turning automatically to the moving sun cannot fail to appreciate their abstract, noiseless, pollutionless beauty both in reality and as symbol. Yet local home owners near the wind farms

81. Marx, p. 365.

in California have attempted to block their visual intrusion to protect their outdated nostalgia for a vanished pastoralism expressed in their Cape Cod subdivisions. This is a serious philosophical issue that raises basic questions about our image of the gardens and the man-made landscape. The "new symbols of possibility" that eluded pioneers at the beginning of this century are yet to be found across the distant grounds that call for change.

Le Parc de la Villette,
Bernard Tschumi
(see pages 194–199)

Hidcote

Lawrence Johnston

1. Miles Hadfield, *A History of British Gardening*, 3rd ed. (London: Humanities, 1979), p. 427.

2. Ann Scott-James, *Sissinghurst* (London: Michael Joseph, 1975), p. 40.

3. William Morris, "The Lesser Arts," in *Hopes and Fears for the Arts* (London: Ellis & White, 1878).

Hidcote and Sissinghurst, the quintessential English gardens of this century, exist as legendary names independent of their reality. Gardeners from all over the world make pilgrimages to Gloucestershire and Kent to see these gardens they have read and heard so much about, and they are not disappointed. Each garden is rooted in a particular place, Hidcote on the north escarpment of the Cotswolds, Sissinghurst in the Weald of Kent. They could not be anywhere else than the very depths of England. Although remote, rural, domestic in scale, both gardens reflect the worldly sophistication and intelligence of their creators, giving them their universal appeal. Each is, as Miles Hadfield wrote of Hidcote, "'the perfectest figure' of twentieth century gardens."[1]

Vita Sackville-West, who with her husband, Harold Nicolson, made Sissinghurst and was deeply affected and influenced by the older Cotswold garden, only vaguely mentions meeting its creator, Lawrence Johnston, "long ago" in an essay she wrote for the *Royal Horticultural Society Journal* in 1949. And there is no certain evidence of the Nicolsons' having visited Hidcote until 1941, ten years after they had begun their work at Sissinghurst.

Hidcote, begun in 1905, twenty-five years before the Nicolsons acquired the dilapidated castle in Kent, has often been linked to Sissinghurst in gardening philosophy and as a visual experience. Johnston's clear, decisive, and forthright plans for Hidcote no doubt appealed to Harold Nicolson's own convictions that a garden designer "must have a sketch map clear in his head before he starts to level or plant."[2]

Like Sissinghurst, no garden existed at Hidcote Bartrim Manor when Johnston first began his work with such American self-confidence. The old Cotswold farmhouse of buff stone and a roof of stone shingles presided over a group of sturdy barns and outbuildings, some fields, and a few clumps of ancient beeches, nothing more. It was a setting of picturesque charm one might have found at the turn of the century where a dedicated Arts and Craft community would be toiling away under the leadership of William Morris as he preached the gospel of art by and for the people. An undistinguished, windswept piece of ground, the site was without any obvious advantages except its intensely understated and romantic Englishness, a quality much sought after in the wake of the ravages of the Industrial Revolution. Before you arrive, the English character of the place is established in vignettes that could have been recorded in a well-bred watercolor of the nearby villages, the picturesque thatched cottages and hamlet lining the way up the plateau to the manor's entry gate. In the beginning nothing about the shape of the land or its particular "genius" suggested a direction or even a Popeian consultation for the development of a garden.

Although he was an American by birth, Johnston adopted characteristic English reticence regarding his personal tastes, and he has left us few clues to his gardening philosophy as a result. Yet a passage on the English landscape from Morris's "The Lesser Arts" comes to mind when considering the appeal the manor must have had for Johnston when he first saw it: "Not much for swelling into hugeness;…no great wastes overwhelming in their dreariness, no great solitudes of forests, no terrible untrodden mountain walls; all is measured, mingled, varied, gliding easily one thing into another, little rivers, little plains…little hills, little mountains…neither prison nor palace, but a decent home."[3]

Vita Sackville concluded that the flawless originality of Hidcote's garden lay outside the restraints of precise genealogy when it came to sorting out the sources of influence on Hidcote's design and development. But Hidcote, like Sissinghurst and a number of the gardens worked on together by the partners Edwin Lutyens and Gertrude Jekyll between 1893 and 1910, suggests a close family kinship that is peculiarly English. Even though Johnston brought together the principal traditions and styles of English gardening in a brilliantly orchestrated creation, there are other English qualities that were also essential ingredients in shaping Hidcote.

First of all, the Nicolsons and Johnston were resolutely amateurs in their background, philosophy, and style, a quality Sir Nikolaus Pevsner has identified as characteristically English. It is the amateur, not the professional or specialist, who has played a large role in English cultural and political life "from maiden aunts to Prime Ministers," and it is a quality particularly valued in the field of architecture and landscape design. Stourhead, that masterwork of the eighteenth century, was largely the creation of its owner, Henry Hoare II. Edwin Lutyens had no formal training as an architect, and Miss Jekyll was a lady of means who could not be regarded as a serious professional earning her living through art. Maintaining one's amateur status seems always to have been a part of the English idea of good breeding. In the eighteenth century, no gentleman would admit to a professional calling outside the church or the law. When it came to painting, architecture, or landscape design, he was expected to know enough to know what he wanted, but not enough to be accused of being an aesthete or intellectual. As for the skills of gardening, the climate and the geography encouraged everyone to garden much as picturesque nature invited everyone to become a Sunday painter. Even today, highly knowledgeable gardeners will pretend a certain diffidence that belies their well-earned skills, a characteristic quite apparent at the annual Chelsea Flower Show in London.

Great Dixter is another surviving garden from the period expressing the same garden philosophy and style of living, yet uniquely its own. Like Hidcote it, too, was an obscure manor house without a garden ("an agricultural property with farmhouse attached") when it was bought by Nathaniel Lloyd in 1910. Even though Lloyd became a self-made architectural historian and student of gardening, he carefully maintained his amateur standing. He engaged Lutyens to remodel the house and to assist him in laying out the garden that was further developed and made famous by his son, Christopher Lloyd.

All of these gardens are modest in scale, at least by the opulent standards of the Edwardian Age. But scale, except in the illusion of modesty, like those other revered English qualities of comfort and good sense, has little to do with it. It is risky, also, to link genealogically the appreciation of simple rural landscape settings espoused by the politically motivated Arts and Crafts movement to Johnston or to Lutyens and Jekyll. In picturesque planting details and in the incorporation of rustic farm structures as background, their work was sympathetic to the aesthetic values of William Morris and his followers. However, Jekyll and Lutyens believed strongly in formal, architectonic principles. And by no stretch of definition could Hidcote's eleven acres be called a cottage garden, even though Johnston, like Jekyll, appreciated and borrowed the casual improvisation of the English vernacular gardener in a number of the small enclosures where plants grow in abandoned order.

To visualize Hidcote's design, Miles Hadfield's description of the plan cannot be improved upon:

The rising land was levelled and ascended from time to time by flights of steps; it was enclosed by a variety of hedges, and formed in a series of geometrically designed gardens, each with its own delights, such as gazebos or pleached limes. All are symmetrically placed on axis with a clear vista through, ending in the piers of a fine gateway.

The valley was turned into a wild garden; a path winds above the stream, which is shadowed by rare trees, its banks planted with shrubs, lilies, primulas, and other naturalized plants. This little valley diverges somewhat from the main axis of the vista, and it is in this broadening space that we see the true genius of design, for it is packed with a number of little hedged apartments into which one descends, each different and each a place of enchantment.[4]

4. Hadfield, pp. 427-428.

Johnston was a botanist and plantsman and did not consider himself a garden designer except to "recognize that the foundations of any good English garden" as Harold Nicolson wrote, "are water, trees, hedges, and lawn....Our superb climate conditions our style." A Cotswold wind and an indifferent soil aside, Johnston made the most of the congenial climate, which allowed him to introduce exotic plants, shrubs and trees gathered on his wide travels. Hadfield concludes, "Here the ancient world of China and the Mediterranean lie side by side, as do happily those once bitter enemies, nature and formality."[5]

4. Hadfield, p. 427.

By breaking up the space along its main lines with tall hedges rather than walls and gates, the Hidcote garden maintains the illusion of easy communication while deepening in surprises, as in a maze, the feeling of secrecy, a quality the Nicolsons admired and Harold called a masterful "fusion of expectation with the element of surprise."[6] Here again Johnston may have vaguely had in mind the linked enclosures of a Tudor garden, but the reference is transformed with a forward-looking vitality and conviction that eludes historical quotation in both architecture and in landscape design.

6. Ibid.

Although the classic English Palladian house of the eighteenth century held little surprise in the cubic clarity of its exterior, the interior was often developed with an unexpected element of surprise, as Pevsner has pointed out. Both William Kent and Robert Adam used columnar screens to conceal the scale and bounds of a room, and John Soane was a master of illusion and surprise in his house in London. So Johnston may have been recalling the lines of Pope:

He gains all points who pleasingly confounds Surprises, varies and conceals the bounds.

Johnston's layout, in its deceptive complication, instinctively proceeded to explore and exploit an old English tradition.

In addition to the established gardening traditions that Johnston so effectively summarized without being overwhelmed at the expense of his own identity, he also addressed the planning and aesthetic problem of how to accommodate the new and appealing plant material that had flooded into England from all parts of the empire throughout the nineteenth century. His introduction of compartments allowed him to adapt random cottage garden methods of planting in order to absorb the number of varieties that interested him, but the overall composition in its calculated scale, texture, and colors translates Hidcote into a masterpiece of garden art.

Old Westbury Gardens
George Abraham Crawley

That killjoy Thorstein Veblen would not have approved. From the dour perspective of his *Theory of the Leisure Class* (1899), extravagant gardens and estates like Old Westbury Gardens had no socially redeeming qualities. Whatever their beauty, gardens were transient affairs of little substance, and the degree of their "cost effectiveness" could not be justified, according to Veblen's depressing arithmetic. We can only be grateful that he did not discourage the Phipps family and others like them who created the country estate garden tradition in America at the turn of the century. Old Westbury, on Long Island's Gold Coast is the best-preserved example to have survived without change.

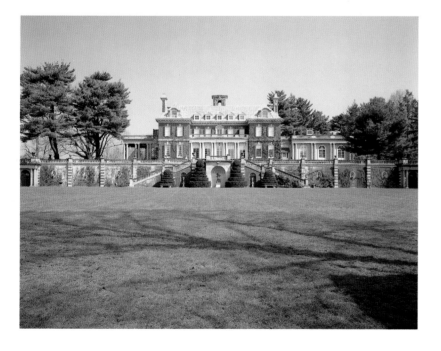

In 1904, the same year that Edith Wharton's *Italian Villas and Their Gardens* was first published, John S. ("Jay") Phipps and his English bride of a year, Margarita C. Grace, embarked on the development of their new estate: approximately two hundred acres of open country on Long Island just above the Hempstead Plain. Both Mrs. Wharton and the Phippses knew European gardens well and were willing to take a few lessons in practice and theory from the traditions of Italy, France, and, of course, England. Mrs. Wharton was appalled by the confusion which then passed for garden taste in America. Her message, thinly disguised in Italianate elegance, was clearly addressed to reform. The fashionable bedding-out of tender flowers in outrageous subtropical colors thrown into patterns more suitable for wallpaper and carpets was an affront to any cultivated sensibility. The formations of cannas, petunias, and dahlias were marked out as if by a drill sergeant rather than a designer of gardens in any recognized tradition of taste. The Phippses clearly shared her concern, for they engaged the English architect George Abraham Crawley to plan their house and grounds at Westbury. The garden remains an astonishing blend of the well-bred English regard for nature and the Frenchman's innate reservations about nature's ultimate reliability. In his commodious geometry the French gardener always leaves no doubt that nature belongs to him. Old Westbury Gardens in its disarming maturity resolves any cultural disagreements between the two points of view.

Crawley's red-brick manor house was inspired by the English country house of the late seventeenth century. But for all its formal elegance and splendid detailing both inside and out, Westbury House is saved from forbidding correctness by its cosmopolitan landscaped setting.

Grounds for Change

The site had been a secluded nest of small farms for more than two centuries. Their consolidation into large estates at the turn of the present century moved with about the same speed as the breakup of the countryside today for subdivisions. Of some fifty Quaker farms in the Westbury community in 1896, only three were left by 1903. The open fields, meadows, and low, wooded hills quickly became the preserve of another group who, like the Quakers, wanted a world of their own. Barely visible in a 1913 photograph of the north lawn of the Phipps house is the newly planted beech allée looking as parvenue as the steel money not long since arrived from the Pittsburgh mills. Time and more money gave both the new garden and a new fortune a finished dignity.

The gardens are laid out along a grand network of axes within a large, romantic English park. Breathtaking vistas are carefully manipulated by the astonishing range of greens in summer and gold to black-bronze in autumn. But despite the impressionistic views recalling the English landscape school of Lancelot ("Capability") Brown and Humphry Repton, the combined effect of the house and grounds is the result of an integrated, formal design. It was just such coordination that Edith Wharton identified as fundamental to Renaissance gardens, and it is a principle advanced by Beaux Arts design theory that American architects and landscape designers like Charles Adams Platt and Beatrix Jones Farrand successfully used in their work.

1. Blomfield, p. 2.

A few years before Mr. and Mrs. Phipps started on their grand plan, Frederick Law Olmsted visited London and reported that the English garden profession—architects, their clients, landscape designers, and estate gardeners— were in one of its periodic wars over issues of landscape design. Since in the United States there has never been anything approaching an established garden tradition worthy of a fight or even an argument, these arcane garden battles are difficult for American gardeners to follow. The lines were drawn between the Renaissance revival architect Sir Reginald Blomfield and the natural-garden enthusiast William Robinson. Blomfield, whose book *The Formal Garden in England* appeared in 1892 (during the same decade that George Crawley began his architectural studies), urged that gardeners return to first principles of Beaux Arts design, giving the architect the ultimate control over the landscape—"an extension of the principles of design which govern the house to the grounds which surround it."[1] By contrast, Robinson, who was trained as a gardener on an Irish estate, believed that a garden's salvation rested almost exclusively with the horticulture. If the architecture seemed out of place, vines, well-placed trees, and shrubs would mask any awkwardness. Whatever unity there was resulted more from nature's intervention than the architect's. George Crawley knew the work of Blomfield very well, and at Westbury House Blomfield's influence, or at least the formal school he championed so successfully, clearly won out. Like Blomfield, Crawley firmly grasped the architect's separate responsibilities, for the building and for creating an appropriate setting.

2. Wharton, p. 8.

3. Middleton Place, near Charleston, South Carolina, dating from the 1740s (see *Antiques* for April 1979, pp. 779–794), and Biltmore, in Asheville, North Carolina, ca. 1890 (see *Antiques* for April 1980, pp. 855–867), are earlier than Old Westbury Gardens and remain in the families of their creators.

The Walled Garden at Westbury, sometimes called "Italian," is nearly four acres in extent and is reached beyond great banks of rhododendrons, the Lilac Walk, and the Rose Garden. The flower borders of the Walled Garden—distinctly un-Italian—are a mass of color throughout the season, a luxuriant use of flowers that probably would have disturbed Mrs. Wharton. "The Italian garden does not exist for its flowers," she wrote, "…late and infrequent adjunct to its beauties, a parenthetical grace counting only as one more touch in the general effect of enchantment."[2] The herbaceous borders at Old Westbury were no doubt the pride of the English Margarita Phipps and a personal, nostalgic touch that most successful gardens manage to include. If there is any conspicuous legacy of William Robinson's garden philosophy at Old Westbury, it is these borders, an element that Robinson first resurrected from the forgotten English cottage garden and then proceeded to turn into an international fashion. He was, of course, greatly helped in the propaganda war by the redoubtable Gertrude Jekyll, whose own incomparable flower borders became a signature for the gardens she designed for Edwin Lutyens.

The quality that gives the garden and house at Old Westbury their rare—if not unique in America—atmosphere is the unbroken attention and devotion of one family for nearly ninety years, even though the estate has been shared with the public for more than a third of that time. To Europeans this hardly seems worthy of note, especially to Englishmen, whose civilized National Trust has allowed families to remain involved in their historic properties even though the properties are now essentially public. Yet in the American country estates there are hardly a dozen houses and almost no gardens with long, uninterrupted family connections.[3]

One of Mrs. Wharton's landscape descriptions in her novel *Twilight Sleep* (1927) captures the feeling of driving into Old Westbury Gardens on a spring morning even now: "Seventy-five thousand bulbs this year! she thought as the motor swept by the sculpted gateway, just giving and withdrawing a flash of turf sheeted with amber and lilac, in a setting of twisted and scalloped evergreens."

Villa Vizcaya
Diego Suarez

The gardens of the Renaissance palace of Vizcaya overlook Biscayne Bay, south of Miami. The house and grounds were designed as a retreat from the winter blasts off Lake Michigan in Chicago, where its builder, James Deering, had spent most of his life. He had searched for years to find the right warm place to spend winters. With a fortune made by his father in the manufacture of farm implements, the middle-aged, midwestern businessman, who had retired because of various ailments, launched the work at Vizcaya in 1912–13, completing it four years later in 1916, when the bay-front property was assembled. He was, in his late, prosaic bachelorhood, an unlikely candidate to have built what is surely the best sixteenth-century garden in America.

The impenetrable tangles of hammock jungle on the western shores of the bay that Deering chose as the site for his garden and palace were some four miles south of Miami. It was then a small fishing village where most people lived off the rich northerners who came in season to stay at Henry Flagler's Royal Poinciana Hotel, built when the Florida East Coast Railway arrived, in 1896. Deering's father, William, had retired to nearby Coconut Grove a few years earlier, after merging his company with International Harvester. When James's own retirement followed in 1910, the younger Deering quickly made plans to leave the chill and the industrial strife of Chicago for the life of a cultivated gentleman in the tropics. He had methodically studied the world's winter climates in Africa, Spain, France, Italy, and California and concluded that Florida's mean temperature of 75 degrees Fahrenheit was ideal. All he needed was a little direction and encouragement, which he was shortly to find.

Paul Chalfin, who had studied painting, was then a young New York protégé of the decorator Elsie de Wolfe. (His allergy to oil paint had caused him to turn to interior decoration.) Deering had met him briefly through Miss de Wolfe and selected him as his impresario for the Florida adventure. Chalfin, in turn, introduced Deering to the young architect F. Burrall Hoffman, who had worked for M. Carrère and Hastings, but skillfully established his own role as the intermediary between client and architect. Chalfin intended to control all aspects of his client's building dreams.

If Deering had any stylistic preference for his winter quarters, it seemed to be drawn vaguely from the Iberian Peninsula. But with Chalfin's manipulation, the focus of the client's interest shifted from Spain to Italy. Without much experience of his own in Italy, Hoffman sensibly took himself off to Venice immediately, in true American fashion, to capture the feel of Italian villas. There, at the suggestion of Chalfin, he visited the Villa Rezzonico in the Veneto north of Venice. Although Hoffman later said that no particular villa was important as inspiration, it was to become something of a model for Vizcaya. In the spring of 1914, guided by his decorator, Deering also decided to absorb the flavor and atmosphere of villa life himself, since nothing in Chicago had prepared him for the new world he planned to create. It was a propitious introduction, for he met Chalfin in Florence, where they stayed with the garden connoisseur Arthur Acton at his villa, La Pietra. Before his departure for Europe, Chalfin had taken care to name himself director of Deering's landscape and gardens so that he could continue to act as the impresario for the entire project. It was fortuitous that their host, Mr. Acton, had turned the Americans over to a young landscape architect, Diego Suarez, who knew the private gardens of Florence, including the Villa Medici, owned by Lady Sybil Cutting. Lady Sybil was a friend of the American novelist Edith Wharton, who in turn would urge Suarez to move to New York where she was sure that the time was right for him to bring some much needed taste to American millionaires. A native of Colombia, Suarez had studied architecture at the Accademia di Belle Arti in Florence and had worked on a number of garden designs in the classical tradition. He had also been involved with the restoration of the gardens at La Pietra. Arthur Acton had retained the French landscape architect Henri Duchêne for several years to carry out the restoration work on his villa and had, according to Suarez, passed on to him Duchêne's restoration ideals and techniques.

When Suarez arrived in New York, the first millionaire (or rather his agent) to turn up was Paul Chalfin who hired the twenty-six-year-old designer in short order to design James Deering's garden in the wilds of South Miami. To begin with, the flat, glaring site itself was daunting, with no counterpart in Italian garden history. Chalfin first thought a French model would be more suitable. And while Edith Wharton's book and that of Charles Adams Platt were advancing American interest in the Italian garden, nothing on the scale of the Vizcaya had yet been attempted.

1. Kathryn Chapman Harwood, *The Lives of Vizcaya* (Miami, Fla.: Banyon Books, 1985).

To steer the client's inclinations away from Spain, as Vizcaya's biographer Kathryn Chapman Harwood has pointed out, Chalfin cleverly persuaded Deering that the trade winds sweeping over Biscayne Bay were just like the winds off the Adriatic and that the Florida jungle recalled an ancient Italian *bosco*.[1] Deering cared deeply for the old trees on his property and insisted that they be incorporated into any landscape plans regardless of their ethnic origins. And he warned that the house and garden must not be so Italian as to be unsympathetic with the tropical landscape of hammock and pine. At first, he opposed any wholesale cutting of trees on the property.

The initial plan called for an artificially built mound with trees approached from the front by two grottoes and a water stairway. But Suarez decided this was too enclosed for the tropics, proposing as an alternative two axes of clipped live oak (*Quercus virginiana*), radiating from the house and opening out in a fan on either side of the central walk and mound. On the mound Suarez placed what he called a "Sicilian view house."

The parterres, extensive and elaborate, were copied from the eighteenth-century garden of La Reggia, at Caserta, east of Naples, designed by Luigi Vanvitelli in 1752 to remind the Spanish Bourbon king of Naples of his French heritage. Suarez even called for the use of colored pebbles and sand, a technique of design elaboration that was definitely French via the Neopolitan Court of Charles III. When Deering learned from his neighbor Mrs. Potter Palmer that because of the salt air she had lost most of the five thousand boxwood used to outline her parterres, he found the low-growing wild jasmine (*Jasminum simplicifolium*) to provide the dark green edge called for in the drawings of his designer.

89   Villa Vizcaya

Suarez finished his setting for the great fountain, discovered in Rome, by surrounding it with a network of waterways. But his most original idea was to transform the awkward breakwater on the bay front of the house into a stone barge folly. The island had emerged from old stumps and rubble left over from dredging, and Deering had imagined it in the shape of a boat—but not too "boaty," avoiding, in his words, being "undignified." Fired with memories of the gardens of Isola Bella on Lake Maggiore and perhaps a forgotten photograph of the marble paddle wheeler built for the last Empress of China, Suarez transformed the nondescript breakwater into a royal barge one hundred and seventy-five feet long and thirty-six feet wide. The teahouse and tropical plantings that once decorated the barge were swept away in the hurricane of 1926. The sculptor Stirling Calder, Alexander Calder's father, who was then working on the sculpture for the Panama-Pacific Exposition in San Francisco, was engaged to do the decoration for the barge. Deering was shocked by Calder's voluptuous figures bearing baskets of fruit and refused to pay for what Calder called his "saucy sea bitches" unless the sculptor altered his "poor sea girls."

The barge and the estate were an immediate hit in the press. The entire issue of the July 1917 *Architectural Review* was devoted to them; seven pages were given to the barge alone, but nowhere was Diego Suarez mentioned. He left his largely unacknowledged association with Chalfin not long after the completion of Vizcaya and returned to New York where he practiced architecture. It was not until Chalfin omitted Suarez's name forty-five years later in an interview by the *New York Times* and was challenged by Burrall Hoffman that the record was set straight.

Villandry

Dr. Joachim Carvallo

No one has yet identified the first conscious effort to restore or reconstruct a garden, carrying it back through the research and romantic imagination to what is believed to be its original appearance at some remote moment in time. The very fragility and constant change of nature has always made such efforts subject to more speculation and guesswork than the restoration of architecture or painting. In 1775, not long after he had become king, Louis XVI was confronted with the question of what to do with the deteriorating park of Versailles. Some of the trees forming the skeleton of André Le Nôtre's original plan dated back to the seventeenth century. Others were slightly later replacements but set in their historic lines. A few advisers to the king advocated a break with the past and argued for an open, flowing composition reflecting the new style of *le jardin anglais*. The decision to replant more or less according to the general plan laid out for Louis XIV and begun in 1665 may well have resulted in the first major garden restoration.

The restoration and re-creation of the past, attempting to return not only buildings but entire villages and town centers to a semblance of their original appearance is a fine art and a sometime science of the twentieth century. The meticulous restoration work of Henri Duchêne and his son Achille at Vaux-le-Vicomte, Le Marais, and Courances dates from just before the turn of the century. Individual and institutional motivations behind this phenomenon are complex but it is evident that the creation of Villandry's gardens, which might have once been a part of the setting for the surviving Renaissance château, began as an extension of the work to restore the castle and related structures. Since Villandry's garden is not based on any garden that once existed there, nor is it related to any surviving Renaissance plan—indeed, important sections of the garden structure actually date

from the eighteenth century—it must be considered an original work of this century. Joachim Carvallo studied as a scientist and physician before he married the American heiress Ann Colman in 1899. When she came into her inheritance in 1906, the couple decided to retire to the Loire Valley, where in 1906 they found the dilapidated château.

Villandry lies beside the rivers Cher and Loire a few miles west of Tours in the Touraine. As restored, the château now appears much as it did when it was built by Jean Lebreton, who served as secretary of state to François I between 1533 and 1545. France was on its way to transforming the Italian style it had just discovered into its own image. François had invited Sebastiano Serlio, an Italian architect, to work in France in 1540. Serlio's château Ancy-le-Franc introduced the first integrated design of garden and architecture based on Italian architectural theory. At about the same time, Jacques Androuet Du Cerceau had traveled to Italy and on his return published the first architectural handbook by a Frenchman. His later book *Les plus excellents bâtiments de France* (1576 and 1579) comprises the best source of information on French garden design of the sixteenth century. No visual documentation of the original Villandry garden survived, as it had in the restoration of Vaux-le-Vicomte and Courances, so it was to the engravings of Du Cerceau that Dr. Carvallo turned when he created the new gardens or, more particularly, the parterres of the *potager* of Villandry. What most visitors do not recognize is the balanced organization of the layout provided by surviving canals that were actually built in the middle of the eighteenth century with no connection to French garden designs of earlier centuries.

Villandry rests on the foundation of the twelfth-century feudal castle of Colombier and when Lebreton's fashionable château was built, the old keep at the southwest corner, canal, basin, and two sides of the moat were retained. In the seventeenth and eighteenth centuries, when the château and gardens were remodeled, however, "with their mistrust of national tradition and unreflecting preoccupation with the antique," as Dr. Carvallo wrote, the restorers "were no longer able to understand the subtleties of the earlier century and the moat was filled in and classical terraces built. Any vestiges of the original Renaissance gardens were swept away with the insensitivity shown by Capability Brown's leveling of Tudor and Stuart parterres in England."[1] The same thing had happened at Azay-le-Rideau and Chambord and was not corrected until the time of the inventive work at Villandry, when the present gardens were designed.

The bastions forming a massive belvedere against the hill above the east wing survived, as did some terracing and skeletal sections of the masonry. The garden itself is divided by four tiers at different levels of hierarchy that conform to Dr. Carvallo's notions of cultural and aesthetic order as he understood it, particularly after the formerly liberal, free-thinking doctor suddenly turned *"réaction-aire, catholique, clérical,"* in the words of Boni de Castellane. It is from that date that he began in earnest to fulfill his fantasies of correct domestic order and hierarchy. The *Jardin d'Ornament* was completed before 1914, the *potager* between 1914 and 1918. The brilliance of Villandry's garden and Carvallo's intuition derives from the "unhistorical" vitality of the overall composition and the unprecedented use of exotic vegetables that might, in other hands, have turned out as academic, monotonously repetitious, or merely eccentric.

On the terrace next to the south side of the château is the *Jardin d'Ornament*, laid out in four compartments by the Spanish artist Lozano. Hearts, masks, and flames symbolize *l'amour tendre,* while swords and daggers represent *l'amour tragique* and *l'amour folie*. The long, rectangular space, best seen from a window in the château, appears regular and uniform, yet this is an illusion when the complexity of the hedging and paths are studied closely. Lavender and santolina contrast with the dark box.

At the lowest level of the twelve-acre space is the vegetable garden, consisting of nine squares enclosed with low trellises covered with roses at the corners. The pattern of each square is lined out with miniature box, following closely the studied details in Du Cerceau's engravings. Each is planted with a different vegetable. It is in these parterres that Carvallo managed to convey that humanist quality of sensibility by which both art and utility are combined and are made to function together in harmony. Du Cerceau was not a gardener, and it is difficult to determine from his engravings whether vegetables and herbs were in fact planted in elaborate parterres as those now seen at Villandry. Later writers on the French garden, Olivier de Serres, Jean Siébault, and Claude Mollet, of the sixteenth and seventeenth centuries suggest that the intact plan of a *potager* was to be in large, simple squares and not divided into small compartments.

1. Quoted in Christopher Hussey, "Le Château de Villandry," *Country Life* 103, n.p.

Just as the layout of Villandry is original in its subtle incorporation of anachronistic elements, the plantings, too, are inspired. When one considers the seasonal variations of color and texture Carvallo built into the scheme, his subtle imagination as a contemporary garden designer becomes more apparent.

The eighteenth-century canal that joins the restored and earlier castle moat, the main axis of the garden formed by an avenue of limes, the ramps, and the terraces all extend the architecture into the landscape, linking it firmly with the garden. The resulting harmony, so well understood by the French Renaissance and now surviving at Villandry, has a long lineage and ultimately derives from Vitruvian theory. In the twentieth century architects and garden designers have been haunted by their inability to reunite their work with the same creative spirit that marks earlier periods. One lesson to be learned at Villandry is found not just in its composite style or fascinating details, but in the way it reflects the closely knit relationship between the arts and the science of horticulture. It is rare that a new garden in an historical setting, rife with what some would call academic gaffes, is capable of expressing an inner significance that transcends the historical period it was meant merely to represent.

The Viceregal Garden
Sir Edwin Lutyens

The garden of the Viceroy's palace at the heart of Edwin Lutyens's new imperial capital city of New Delhi distills the aesthetic, political, and emotional qualities that have defined this stretch of the Jumna River for centuries. The British were only the latest foreign rulers to occupy this arid—Babur called it charmless—spot, the key to the control of Hindustan.

All of this could, of course, be said of Lutyens's whole imperial scheme to house the King-Emperor's government. But the garden, which carries on the tradition of the Mughal rulers who also saw the garden setting as the ceremonial center of their administration as did the Persians before them, somehow concentrates the essence of so many ancient garden strategies. Yet this is a twentieth-century garden, and for all of its cultural and political genealogy, it is not haunted by old histories or involuntarily invented new ones. The garden, like the architecture, is more than a fusion of East and West. It is an original creation born out of the best of both traditions in which the aesthetic and intellectual are combined to advance the symbolic and political needs of its patrons, to provide "peaceful domination and dignified rule over the traditions and life of India."

The genesis of the new seat of government with its palace and garden was the Delhi Durbar of 1911, where the plan to move the government of India from Calcutta to Delhi was announced. As would be expected for such a momentous commission, there was considerable debate over who should receive it. There was objection in the House of Commons that Lutyens had no experience in town planning, a new discipline that was groping its way. Lutyens was finally named, to be joined by the architect Herbert Baker, to work with the planning committee to carry out the design of the complex. The style of the architecture was to be a brilliant amalgamation of western and Indian themes recalling the earlier Mughal strategy of incorporating elements from the Hindu tradition they, too, had supplanted.

In June of 1912, Lutyens sketched on a piece of stationery a rough but unmistakable scheme of the palace, piazza, and garden, a plan that would change little as the physical details emerged over the next twenty years. The house itself was English Palladian but on a scale that exceeded anything in the eighteenth century. The garden area was only outlined, but its relationship, an extension of the house in the Serlian manner, was to remain.

The ceremonial approach to the palace, stretching three kilometers from its beginning at the War Memorial past the Secretariat blocks, passes through the palace and ends in the garden itself. This position gives the garden its symbolic and emotional weight of time and circumstance without resorting to sheer size. The ultimate hierarchy of the location, like the private audience garden of the Mughal emperor, was manifest. In terms of ceremonial drama, the long approach flanked by canals and lines of ashoka trees, balanced against the concentrated grandeur of the enclosed space subtly elevated above the surrounding plains, is more effective than that of Versailles.

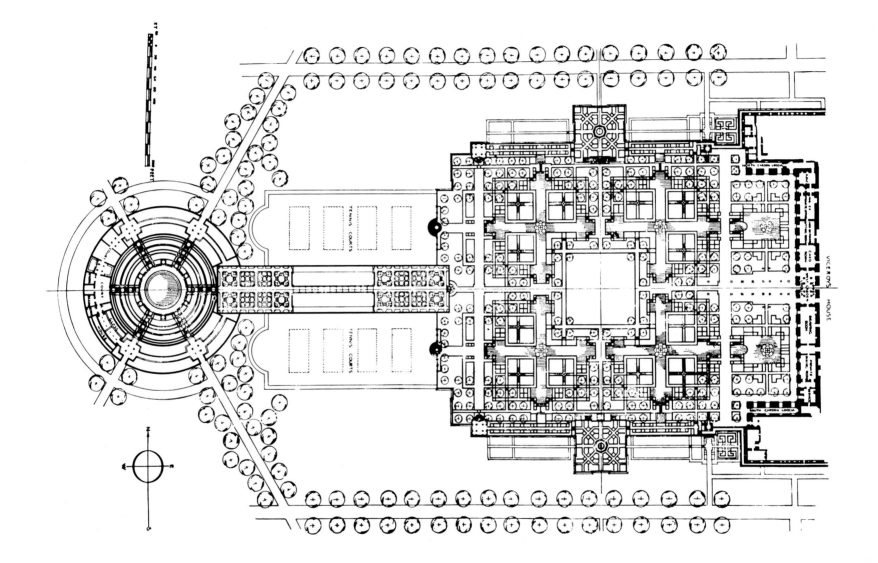

Plan for the Viceregal Garden

The comparison to Versailles is not overstated. When it was completed, Lutyens's palace measured two-thirds of a mile around its foundation and its two hundred thousand square feet was in fact larger than Louis XIV's folly. It assuredly expressed the dream of British imperialism every bit as much as Versailles expressed absolute monarchy or Lutyens's earliest Surrey estates captured the English country house ideal at the turn of the century, as Robert Irving has remarked in his monograph *Indian Summer: Lutyens, Baker and Imperial Delhi.*

The plan for the Viceregal garden was submitted to the Government of India in 1918. In its axial symmetry, the garden is resolutely Ecole des Beaux-Arts in its extension of the architecture. The complex, interlocking geometry of the house itself is repeated in the layout. Its quadripartite plan not only echoes the Muslim geography of Paradise seen in Mughal gardens from Agra to Lahore, but also reflects the spiritual topography of Hebrew and Hindu beliefs.

About the time of the launching of New Delhi, Constance Villers Stuart's pioneer study *Gardens of the Great Mughals* appeared. The book was known to the principals involved in the planning of the capital and in it are reproduced the plans of the garden-palace of Deeg, built in the eighteenth century by the Hindu Raja of Bharatpur. While much simpler in design, there is a similarity in the linked geometry at Deeg that carries a hint of a connection with Lutyens's scheme. Lutyens was capable of just such an obscure Hindu reference in what was called "The Mughal Garden."

The Mughal exultation of water as the central element of their gardens has never been surpassed. Not only does it provide unity, the fountains, chutes, channels, and pools give animation to the flat, static regularity, its emptiness more apparent owing to the often passive viewers sitting in a pavilion or along a terrace. Lutyens understood the theatrical possibilities of water and placed circular fountains of sixteen-tiered lotus leaves carved from sandstone mounted with twelve-foot jets at six key intersections of the canals. At the center of the garden, Lutyens has created a green isle two-hundred-feet square for a garden-party marquee. There are sculpted topiary trees and two striking sandstone gazebos.

Along the garden boundaries the North and South Forts, ninety-feet square, have been placed. The North Fort contains the most remarkable grotto built in this century. Water cascades through a circular opening in the roof of the grotto and falls twenty feet into the square basin below, where a single jet shoots skyward catching the filtered light as it falls back into the pool.

The western end of the public garden is marked by a sandstone screen of large circular openings leading to the tennis courts below. A narrow processional walk some four hundred feet long—dimensions here and throughout the palace complex recall Hadrian's Villa— took the most favored visitor and the Viceroy's family to the Viceroy's private retreat called the butterfly garden. Centered on a calm round pool, tiers of flowers planted on the encircling terraces recall in elevated accents the quiet and peace of an old cottage garden planted by Lutyens's old partner Gertrude Jekyll.

When the Raj was replaced by the new government of India in 1947, the Viceroy's house and garden became the presidential establishment. The bust of "the architect of this house" stands near the great red stone staircase. There are no longer 431 viceregal gardeners, as there were when Lord and Lady Mountbatten departed, but the gardens and ground look earnestly well kept. There are still echos of the past, even if they are not oppressive. Recalling the arrival of the Viceroy with an honored guest as the entourage moved with its spendid mounted guards into the piazza, Robert Byron describes a feeling even the photographs of the period fail to convey:

The whole history of civilized man, of all his politics, his empires, thrones, and wars, of all his efforts to govern and be governed, followed in the soldier's wake. That the entire spectacle, men and buildings, were the symbol of English dominion, seemed merely incidental. But that the evolution of government could demand, and create, in its everyday course such a spectacle seemed to postulate an apotheosis of human order.[1]

The mise-en-scène for that illusion of order had been the vision and imagination of one man.

1. Quoted from an article by Robert Byron, *Architectural Review* (January 1931), reprinted in Michael Alexander, ed., *Delhi and Agra: Travellers' Companion Series* (New York: Atheneum, 1987), p. 150.

Dumbarton Oaks

Beatrix Farrand

Few gardens of this century have achieved the condition of myth. Twentieth-century gardens with a mythic aura are mostly confined to vanished masterpieces like the house of Luis Barragán at El Pedregal and the Guevrékian garden at the Villa Noailles in Provence. The popularity and extraordinary preservation of Sissinghurst and Hidcote by the English National Trust has helped to elevate them to allegory. Maybe it was Igor Stravinsky's Dumbarton Oaks Concerto, commissioned by Mildred and Robert Bliss on their thirtieth wedding anniversary in 1938, that added, by chance, the transcendent ingredient. After all, few gardens have received such a singular honor as to have their name immortalized in music. Or maybe the charmed international life of the Blisses themselves, who commissioned Dumbarton Oaks and fixed its name as a center of cultivation between the wars, simply endowed it with their own legendary reputation of cultivation and glamour. Certainly their informed taste in music and recherché interests in Coptic textiles, Visigothic bronzes, and Peruvian gold raised their Georgetown establishment to a level not to be found in the run-of-the-mill millionaire estates of the Gatsby era.

Besides pre-Columbian art and Byzantine artifacts, early passions of her husband's that she came to share, Mildred Bliss's own interests were also advanced and perceptive, as Marcel Proust noted in a letter to their mutual friend Madame Sheikevitch in 1918: *"J'ai croisé l'autre jour votre amie Madame Bliss chez Madame Hennessy mais trop rapidement pour pouvoir lui parler de vous. Pas assez cependant pour qu'elle ne m'ait demandé un renseignement littéraire."* "I met your friend Madame Bliss at the home of Madame Hennessy the other day but too briefly to be able to speak of you—long enough, however, for her to ask me about things literary."[1] Gardening and landscape architecture, including

their documented history in books over the centuries, were other interests not widely held at the time.

When the Blisses bought the twenty-two acre property in 1920, the original shell of the federal house had been obscured by dowdy later additions. As for the grounds, their chief distinction was the great oaks, maples, and tulip poplars that shaded the rolling slopes running sharply down into the valley of Rock Creek. Large clumps of ancient boxwood and a greenhouse dating from 1810 gave the generous but run-down lawns around the house an old-fashioned southern air befitting its patrician neighborhood on a hill just to the north of the old port of Georgetown.

Beatrix Jones Farrand, the niece of Edith Wharton, who was a friend of the Blisses, was one of the major American landscape architects when she was invited to visit them shortly after their new acquisition. Following her study with Charles Sprague Sargent, a family friend and head of the Arnold Arboretum of Harvard University, Farrand had established her practice in New York in 1896. The summer before, she had taken Sargent's advice and spent several months in Europe to see the major garden monuments of Italy as well as of England, where she found the relative merits of garden styles a hotly debated subject.

1. Walter M. Whitehill, *Dumbarton Oaks: The History of a Georgetown Home and Garden 1800–1966* (Cambridge: Harvard University Press, 1967), p. 60.

The work of Gertrude Jekyll, a friend of William Robinson's, was also becoming well known at the time, and it was perceptive of Farrand in 1895 to visit Penshurst, a place admired by Jekyll where the ancient Tudor garden had recently been "confirmed and renewed." Farrand absorbed the English artist's pictorial ways with design and her respect for the architectonic bones, which Farrand would later perfect in her own garden designs, notably at Dumbarton Oaks. The terraces at Penshurst, with their brick walls, tall gate piers, and classical urns, had been softened by impressionistic use of colors in the borders, and this, too, had appealed to the American student. Later, the topography of Dumbarton Oaks was to prove much more interesting than the flat Kentish landscape of Penshurst, but the old, picturesque setting of the English estate, with its antique trees carefully respected within the framework of walks, terraces, and masonry, would be echoed in Farrand's work for the Blisses in Washington.

Farrand began her work in 1922, and Mildred Bliss later recalled that the commission was one of the most challenging she had ever taken on. Farrand was confronted with "an existing and a rather dominating house and an unusually wide variety of grades." Even more problematic were "the very definite personal preferences of the owners with their special interest in design and texture."

2. Ibid., p. 65.

3. Wharton, p. 8.

The Blisses clearly outlined their program and garden requirements, for their travels and wide interests gave them well-settled ideas about what they wanted. "The gardens were to be for spring and autumn enjoyment and in winter were to have perennial green in abundance. A swimming pool, tennis court, and brook completed the illusion of country life."[2] Farrand proceeded thoughtfully and, according to Mrs. Bliss, never imposed an arbitrary concept on the land, "listening" to the special genius of the light, wind, and particularly the roll of the ground itself, as the garden evolved over the years. It was to be a brilliant collaboration between strong, experienced, and dynamic personalities.

Aside from Gertrude Jekyll's influence in the use of color and in the planning of the herbaceous borders, Farrand's tastes and that of her clients were conservative and formalist when it came to organization, as Diane McGuire has pointed out. She was greatly influenced by the revival of classical garden traditions as advocated by her aunt Edith Wharton in her book *Italian Villas and Their Gardens*. Some of Wharton's passages could be applied to Dumbarton Oaks without alteration:

The inherent beauty of the garden lies in the grouping of its parts—in the converging lines of its long ilex-walks, the alternating of open spaces with cool woodland shade, the proportion between the terrace and the bowling green, or between the height of a wall and the width of the path....The great pleasure grounds...are laid out on severe majestic lines: the parts are few, the total effect is one of breadth and simplicity.[3]

Thomas Mawson, the English garden designer whose book *The Art and Craft of Garden Making* went through five editions between 1900 and 1926, was also influential and can be detected in Farrand's handling of terraces and steps on the steep slopes of Dumbarton Oaks. Mildred Bliss was particularly interested in garden ornament and details. It was a skill that Farrand observed closely in England and translated successfully into a setting that offered endless opportunities by carefully integrating the decorative element with a deft use of ground covers of Baltic ivy (*Hedera helix*) and *Vinca minor*. The use of vines on balustrades, pergolas, walls, and well-heads had become a fashionable garden detail in the 1930s, and Farrand knew how to introduce wisteria, ivy, and climbing roses without creating a jungle. There was, as McGuire has observed, a conscious respect for the architectural elements, establishing a clear line between the wall plants and the architecture, never obscuring facades and stone details.

This respect for architecture is made explicit in Farrand's directions for the planting of the Green Terrace:

On the east wall of the drawing room are espaliered *Magnolia grandiflora*, which have to be controlled with considerable skill so that they do not become too insistent and enveloping. Some heavy planting, however, is useful in masking the awkward angle between the corner of the connecting passageway….This is a small re-entering angle, which if not filled with foliage, makes an unfortunate line.[4]

Along with their friendship over the years, "the gardens grew naturally from one another," Mildred Bliss wrote in her tribute to Beatrix Farrand, "until now in their luxuriant spring growth, as in the winter when leafless branches show each degree of distance and the naked masonry…there is a special quality of charming restfulness."[5] Dumbarton Oaks had taken on its own unique, mythic personality born out of the knowledge, imagination, and wisdom of its creator and of the civilized ideals of her patrons.

4. McGuire, *Beatrix Farrand's Plant Book for Dumbarton Oaks*, p. 32.

5. Whitehill, p. 67.

The Cactus Garden, Huntington Botanical Gardens

William Hertrich

The Cactus Garden of the Huntington Botanical Gardens began as and remains a horticultural collection set out on the estate of the California financier Henry E. Huntington. Even though its creator, William Hertrich, had studied landscape design, his background and interests were in horticulture when Huntington hired him in 1904 to take charge of his new San Marino estate near Pasadena. What Hertrich seems instinctively to have understood was the living architecture of the cactus in all its forms—round, flat, horizontal—some reaching up twenty to thirty feet and weighing more than five tons. Huntington's commission was an unprecedented opportunity in the Golden Age of great private gardens in America, and Hertrich was prepared to make the most of it, particularly when it came to his passion for the cactus family.

Having accumulated a major fortune, in part from the development of the new city of Los Angeles, Henry Huntington was ready to build a house for his growing art and book collection, with extended landscaped grounds appropriate to his new wealth and pursuits, which included gardening. In 1903, Huntington bought the San Marino Ranch, overlooking the beautiful San Gabriel Valley as the site for his estate. To the north stretched a magnificent range of the Sierra Madre mountains. Even now it is breathtaking to contemplate the speed with which these "instant" estates were created with limitless budgets and energy to fuel the enterprise. This miraculous transformation of a landscape where nothing had existed before was part of the formula for conspicuous consumption on the grand scale by the triumphant capitalist at the turn of the century.

Once the architectural firm of Hunt and Grey had prepared their plans and the location for the residence was established, Hertrich plotted his strategy and began his work in earnest. Over eight thousand wagon loads of peat were quickly moved into the planting area around the house. Then Hertrich persuaded his patron to establish greenhouses and nurseries where the collection was able to grow to royal proportions in short order. The new Lath House alone immediately sheltered fifteen thousand plants that were rushed in from all over the world. This international plant collecting on an imperial scale establishes the context for the Cactus Garden, begun as a part of the estate in 1905. Included in this picture are the impressive technological advances that suddenly made such large-scale gardening possible—fast transportation to move large plants and trees over long distances, horticultural skills capable of dealing with exotic plant material that had been moved halfway around the world at maturity, all the techniques of plant hunting inherited from the previous century. Technology, which was to bring such devastation to the natural environment in this century, had also made these singular achievements possible, at least for the very rich and determined.

Grounds for Change

The Huntington Cactus Garden is a horticultural phenomenon linked to an economic and cultural era of private American fortunes where money, imagination, and creative energy along with technology seemed to know no bounds. In fact, the Cactus Garden began as a way to fill the bare space of a barren hillside below the residence where the soil was worn out and where Hertrich claimed only desert plants would grow. Huntington himself had no interest in such a garden at first, claiming that cactus reminded him of the Arizona desert, where he had worked supervising the construction of the Southern Pacific Railroad. In his own realm of horticulture and landscaping, Hertrich was something of an empire builder himself, and countered by proposing that the new desert garden should represent all types of cacti and succulents from all over the world. The desert of Southern California had many species and varieties, of course, while the region of Mexico contained the largest collection in the world. Hertrich personally took charge of the plant-hunting expeditions, shipping carloads back to the new garden.

It is not surprising that within two decades, Henry Huntington had the world's largest collection of desert plants grown out of doors. In the beginning, when William Hertrich's international shipments would suddenly arrive by boat and train, with no design considerations other than pragmatic ones, the collection was set out as a botanical garden, with small beds and narrow, winding paths. During the time that the Huntington family lived on the estate, visitors were rarely admitted to any of the gardens, so the garden-design work was done for the private pleasure of the owner, not to accommodate the public. In the 1920s four additional acres were added to the Cactus Garden, opening up the possibility of using enormous plant specimens, including South African aloes, Mexican yuccas, dasylirions, century plants, and South American cereus. Gradually, the Huntington Cactus Garden became a mecca for serious horticultural students from all over the world.

The enlargement of the garden also made possible the re-alignment of walks and roads for the growing number of visitors. In 1930 a broad central walk ten feet wide and over a thousand feet long was laid down through the center. It was at this time that carloads of lava rock were brought in to create a rockery, anticipating similar rockeries that Roberto Burle Marx would later build in his brilliant gardens in Brazil. A curving driveway separating the Cactus Garden from the Palm Collection was also built to allow an overview of the exotic desert setting below. These modest interventions only enhanced the visitor's ability to study and to appreciate what nature itself had created in this extraordinary horticultural assembly transcending the quotidian conventions and principles of landscape design.

The Cactus Garden, Huntington Botanical Gardens

Naumkeag

Fletcher Steele

Naumkeag, nestled in the middle of the Berkshire hills, was the summer estate—"home" does not quite work—of the lawyer and diplomat Joseph Hodges Choate, who built it in the 1890s. When his daughter, Miss Mabel Choate, finally inherited the estate from her father in 1926 at the restless age of fifty-six, she was ready, willing, and—with the family fortune in the offing—quite able to transform the original setting of the house designed by the young Stanford White. That summer Mabel met the landscape architect Fletcher Steele.

Naumkeag's original garden surrounding the sedate, shingle-and-brick structure had been laid out on the forty-nine acres at the edge of Stockbridge, Massachusetts, by the Boston designer Nathan Barrett. Fletcher Steele admired Barrett's "inspired" vision above that of most landscape designers of that time, who, according to Steele, merely "fumbled." Barrett's results were well-bred if conventional. On the terraces north of the house, for example, he had included two large flower gardens that were distinctly Victorian with their beds of heliotrope and geranium. "Bedding out," then still fashionable, was easy for the Choates, who continued to maintain that essential luxury of the period, a large greenhouse in the country, to supply annuals for the garden and cut flowers year-round for their house in New York City.

Fletcher Steele had been born in Pittsford, New York, and after graduating from Williams College entered the Harvard School of Landscape Architecture in 1907, a year after the inception of the new graduate program. Harvard's training was grounded in the tradition of the Beaux Arts, and its ties to the Architecture School confirmed a strong design tradition in which "materials are subordinated to their arrangements," in the words of James Sturgis Pray, chairman of the department. By the summer of 1926, when Steele was introduced to Mabel Choate after he delivered a lecture to the Garden Club of Lenox, Massachusetts, he was well established as one of the leading landscape architects of the Eastern seaboard.

In addition to his thriving and very grand practice during that Golden Age of American garden building just before and following World War I, Steele had sharpened his critical faculties by teaching, lecturing, and writing. Travel was also important to his development, and annual trips to Europe became essential. As an artist—he considered himself a landscape sculptor—he kept a consciously open mind and sympathy to new ideas. After the important Paris Exposition of 1925 his work took on a bolder, more abstract quality, reflecting the avant-garde garden designs he had seen and admired at the Paris show, as his biographer Robin Karson has pointed out. Garrett Eckbo, Dan Kiley, and others have recognized Steele as "the transitional figure between the old guard and the moderns," in Eckbo's words. Kiley has said that he was "the only good designer working during the twenties and thirties…the only one interested in new things."

Even though something of an iconoclast in his landscape ideas—he once told an admiring audience that Americans lay out "far too large a plan, look at it hopelessly, and then go to the movies"—and freely expressed his horror of the popular, mindless fads that passed for garden design, his "many truths told in so delightful a fashion" seemed to encourage rather than alienate potential well-heeled clients with conservative tastes. For the willful, strong-minded Mabel Choate, Fletcher Steele's worldly sophistication was refreshing. During the next thirty years the unlikely pair—she was fifteen years his senior—would transform Naumkeag together.

Rather than leveling Barrett's work, Steele accepted not only its structure but its settled, comfortable old-fashioned charm. "The old spirit should be followed…the 'feeling' of Victorian elaboration must be continued. Design should be clarified and modern ideas of fitness inaugurated.…Nothing must look up to date."

The first addition was to be the Afternoon Garden, adjacent to the library, a garden space originally inspired by new gardens beginning to appear in the far more congenial climate of California. The house and a new wall fixed two sides of the space, while the south and west sides, opening to a mountain view, needed to be established without blocking the vista. Steele came up with a line of boldly carved and painted oak posts made from pilings salvaged from the Boston Harbor. "Their shape must be good, yet a touch of nonsense would do no harm," he told his client. Ropes enclosing steel cables were festooned between the posts for woodbine and clematis.

121   Naumkeag

Steele's seductive personal charm continued as he outlined his poetic daydream of the imaginary garden that was about to appear: "Dark brick and stone walls; heavy shade from vines and trees; post and statue colorful but dark in tone; rich red purple beech crossing our vision away from the house; dark green banks of foliage beyond. All rather dark. Only the dipping, changing sky for gaiety and cheeriness. We check off the means of raising the color values and enlivening our garden room. We can bring the sky to our feet with a mirror."

Over the next few years Naumkeag's development followed word pictures conjured up by the designer for his willing client. After a terrace to the southwest was built in 1931, Steele persuaded Choate to transform the south lawn, pointing toward Bear Mountain, with a massive, curving earthwork.

"The vital importance of curving form which was begun on the south lawn here at Naumkeag, generated by the curve of Bear Mountain beyond and made clear in the curve cut in the woodland, was a satisfactory experiment," Steele later wrote. "So far as I know it was the first attempt that has ever been made to incorporate the form of background topography into foreground details in a unified design."

The alternative and conventional solution for organizing such a large space and uniting it with the mountainscape would have been some kind of walk leading down the slope and into the woods. But "neither the client nor her Victorian house; neither Bear Mountain nor the hillside itself wanted a so-called naturalistic affair with a path meandering downhill," Steele recalled in a characteristic aside. A range of Italianate terraces would have been just as awkward, since there was nothing remotely Italian about the rolling lawn or Bear Mountain. Besides, Steele argued, a Victorian house in western Massachusetts would look absurd with an Italian garden, ignoring the fact that two years before he had inserted a vista he called "The Perugino View" that might have come from a Maxfield Parrish painting.

At this stage, the landscape architect became a sculptor, creating "an abstract form in the manner of modern sculpture, with swinging curves and slopes which would aim to make their impression directly, without calling on the help of associate ideas, whether in nature or in art."

Even though Steele never gave up his interest in historical quotations and theatrical references in much of his work, especially for clients who shared his taste for allusion and decoration, he was seriously concerned with modern design not as a style but in its more fundamental implications for the future of landscape architecture. He summarized his analysis in an essay, "Landscape Design for the Future," and in his contribution to the exhibition catalogue *Contemporary Landscape Architecture and Its Sources* published by the San Francisco Museum of Art in 1937.

All quotations are from Karson, *Fletcher Steele, Landscape Architect.*

In 1938 Steele made the first plans for "The Blue Steps," his last project at Naumkeag, which he originally had called "the backstairs to the greenhouse." They remain his signature image for Mabel Choate's garden and one of the most memorable elements of an American garden of the twentieth century. The native white birch trees that were to inspire an important part of the composition already grew on the steep hillside before Steele presented his first sketch. He later planted more, graduating their size to replicate a natural grove. Four arches for the stairs were placed equidistant on the slope. Curved-pipe railings painted white with semicircular guardrails placed on each of the landings give the steps that essential "hint of movement, of grace promised, of beauty that hides or lies forgotten," as Steele once wrote of garden stairs. "It is the curve of the back of a leopard made clear in the rail," a quality that hardly needs spelling out at Naumkeag.

A low dark green hedge of *taxus* was planted behind the white railings to make them stand out and further resonate with the birch grove. Aside from introducing a channel of water beneath the arches, intended to be heard more than seen, the final touch was to paint the steps blue.

Starting out with a well-bred, if extravagant, addition to his friend's estate, the artist managed to transform the initial plan through calculation and brilliant improvisation into an evocative creation unique in American landscape design.

The Governor's Palace

Arthur A. Shurcliff

Inventing history was not a discovery of the twentieth century, but no century has shown more professional skill in the reshaping of the past to fit its ideal vision. When John D. Rockefeller, Jr., launched plans to re-create the colonial town of Williamsburg, Virginia, through restoration and reconstruction of an entire environment, the representation of this idealized historical fabric, including the gardens and landscape, assumed a new and influential role in American cultural life.

No one denies that the decision in 1926 to reconstitute the colonial past through the architecture and gardens of a forgotten Virginia village was an act of selective historical revision. Nor could those individuals behind Colonial Williamsburg have anticipated the enormous impact their program would have on American taste in houses, their furnishings, and their gardens. Unlike the buildings, many of which survived or could be rebuilt from archeological evidence, the historical landscape of the eighteenth century, except in a few forgotten corners, had largely disappeared. When Arthur Shurcliff was put in charge of reconstructing the garden setting, there was neither precedent for his role nor an established methodology to follow. Yet, strangely, the work of Colonial Williamsburg's chief landscape architect, who created some of America's most satisfying and influential gardens and town landscapes, has been largely ignored.

The objective of those in charge of the restoration was to compose a beautiful yet cohesive portrait of the imagined American past. The agreed-upon vision was to be that of a Golden Age, an immaculate townscape adorned with brick and clapboard houses in shaded streets and all within a green framework—a picture of a past that was "always blissfully harmonious," as Charles Hosmer, Jr., has written. It was just as well that the later American fetish for obsessive restoration accuracy had not yet surfaced among professional preservationists. Garden archaeology and meticulous documentary research was in its infancy, and although Shurcliff and his staff did visit a number of surviving early gardens scattered in the Virginia countryside, and attempted some documentary analysis to bolster their planning decisions, they were not seriously inhibited by physical or documentary evidence that would clash with the imaginative setting they were determined to create. It was an attitude that would come to be deplored in sound architectural restoration and in garden reconstruction once the state of knowledge and sophistication advanced in this field. But judged from the perspective of the mature results, Williamsburg's early landscape planning more than mitigates the intellectual indiscretions innocently perpetrated.

Arthur Shurcliff (he had changed his name from Shurtleff in 1930) held degrees from both Massachusetts Institute of Technology and Harvard University and was working for the City of Boston in 1928, when the architects Perry, Shaw, and Hepburn, who were responsible for the building of Mr. Rockefeller's new town, engaged him to take charge of its landscape and garden development. His job was to provide a plausible, attractive setting for the architecture of the colonial era.

By the end of the nineteenth century, the Virginia economy had sufficiently revived from the Civil War to encourage a new generation to build or restore houses and to create gardens on a scale that surpassed the Golden Age of the early eighteenth century. Westover, William Byrd II's manor house on the James River, had recovered from war damage thanks to the money and effort of an executive of a steamship company. Monticello was being slowly returned to its original Jeffersonian lines by the Levy family of Philadelphia. Mount Vernon had since 1858 been in care of its Ladies' Association. The fact that the plans and extensive documentation existed for the gardens of both Mount Vernon and Monticello attracted scholarly interest to the subject, but the garden re-creations for the most part were impressionistic, haphazard affairs at both estates. In 1923, the James River Garden Club published *Historic Gardens of Virginia*, which contained conjectural plans of gardens that had long since disappeared. This valuable but neglected book no doubt had an impact on the restoration pioneers of Williamsburg.

Shurcliff was both single-minded and persuasive in his arguments with the architects about the garden designs he proposed. In their interpretive character it is fair to say that they can be viewed as original twentieth-century gardens we now label as Colonial Revival.

The largest and most complex of Shurcliff's compositions is the garden of the Governor's Palace. A nondescript modern high school occupied the original site of the vanished Palace when Rockefeller first visited Williamsburg in the nineteen twenties. A playing field sprawled over the eight acres Shurcliff was charged with recovering and he approached the daunting challenge with his usual energy and imagination.

Except for some primitive outlines in a crude English engraving from the 1740s and a few artifacts recovered on the site, almost nothing was known of the gardens Lieutenant Governor Alexander Spotswood laid out around 1715 after he arrived in the colony in 1710. Spotswood also added a ballroom to the rear of the new building, and it was assumed that some kind of garden existed outside this extension. The upper garden, dominated by the ballroom wing is symmetrical, divided by a central axis with geometric parterres on either side of the broad walk. A lower garden separated by an iron gate and grill is also laid out with parterres, but less elaborately. The cross-axis of American beech (*Fagus grandifolia*) forms a tunnel on the far side of the space. Beyond, an English "visto" has been cut into the wooded park where the top of an occasional truck or train can be glimpsed in the sunken roadbed running through the meadow. A member of the research department warned the architects at the time that there was "no remote possibility that this 'Park' area was ever used for anything except a cow pasture. So any attempt to landscape it would…rob the Palace lay-out of a good deal of verisimilitude." But Shurcliff won the day. The juxtaposition of the geometric order of the enclosed parterred garden with the picturesque park that carries in its seemingly off-handed perspective the central axis into the natural landscape is one of the memorable passages of Shurcliff's work.

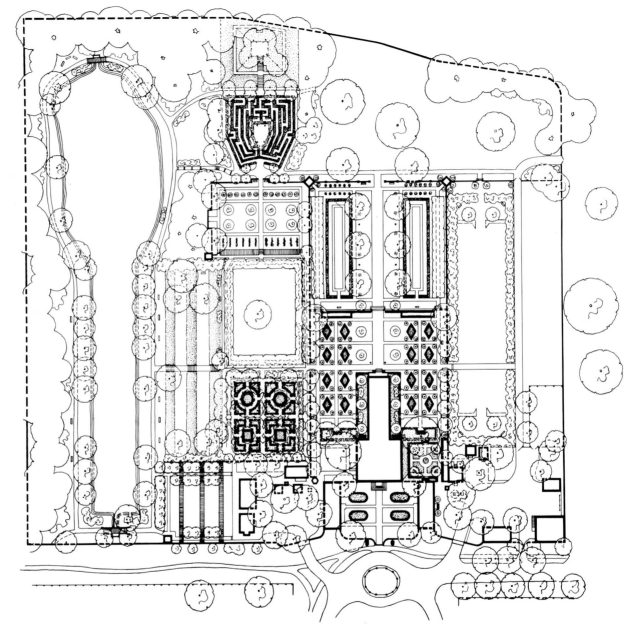

Albert M. Koch's 1960s drawing derived from Arthur A. Shurcliff's 1935 "General Plan for Governor's Palace Approaches, Gardens and Park"
(Colonial Williamsburg Foundation)

Because so little garden history of the colonial period had been undertaken at the time of the original planning at Williamsburg, Shurcliff turned to England and English sources for inspiration. But in fact no Anglo-Dutch gardens of the early eighteenth century had survived in the British Isles, so many of his ideas were extrapolated from Edwardian interpretations and from literary sources. Shurcliff's biggest fight was over his proposal to create a maze and an adjoining mound. When he was unable to document the precedent for a maze either in Williamsburg or in Virginia, he told the architects that the "authenticity of mazes in England at our period is a more important matter for us to consider than mazes in Virginia at the time," once again winning the argument.

As for the restoration of the terraces lining the slope above the canal Spotswood had carved out of the deep ravine west of the property, here Shurcliff was on sounder historical ground, and the way he incorporated this feature into the overall scheme is both convincing and brilliant, transcending the meager record. Indeed, throughout the town and particularly behind the more modest houses south of Duke of Gloucester Street, Shurcliff has taken advantage of the steep depressions with consummate imagination, oblivious to any historical "correctness."

Aside from the great national parks in the west, it can be argued that the gardens created by Colonial Williamsburg beginning in the second quarter of this century are among the few truly original American contributions to the landscape design tradition. I would agree with J. B. Jackson that in both the so-called natural environment of Yosemite National Park and in the re-created gardens of Williamsburg, we have invented uniquely twentieth-century monuments that seem to serve needs special to our time. The garden of the Governor's Palace brings back an imagined past in all its aesthetic richness to challenge a squalid contemporary world. And as Jackson concluded in his essay *The Necessity for Ruins*, "there is no lesson to learn, no covenant to honor; we are charmed into innocence and become part of the environment."[1]

1. Jackson, *The Necessity for Ruins and Other Topics*, p. 102.

The Olivo Gomes Estate
Roberto Burle Marx

No other garden designer in this century has produced as large and as significant a body of work as has the Brazilian master Roberto Burle Marx. Growing up in a country where the riches of nature seem to respect no bounds, producing some fifty thousand species of plants and flowers, Burle Marx found his creative imagination amply supplied but never overwhelmed with the basic material of landscape architecture. Because of his extensive work and the wide range of design issues he has addressed—from great city parks like Flamengo Park in Rio de Janeiro to small, intimate private gardens—it is purely subjective and arbitrary to single out one work as representative of or towering above all the rest. The work of nearly sixty years is far too complex to be labeled merely *O stilo Burle Marx* even though his signature has been recognizable from the very beginning of his career.

The Brazilian architect Lúcio Costa, Burle Marx's earliest mentor and teacher, advised the young painter then moving into landscape design not to call himself a gardener, realizing how little respect that profession commanded. While the young architects in Burle Marx's circle were reacting to the dictates of the Beaux Arts school of architecture and design that had dominated South America for nearly a century, landscape architecture was a warmed-over pastiche imported from Europe.

In 1922, ten years before Burle Marx received his first commission—a roof garden for a small, contemporary house in Rio de Janeiro—some young Brazilian architects and writers announced a cultural and aesthetic revolution during Modern Art Week in São Paulo. Manifestos are seldom able to move artists or cultural establishments to shift directions, but a spark did ignite with remarkable speed. By the beginning of the 1930s Brazil was astonishing the world with its daring new buildings, particularly in its two major cities of Rio de Janeiro and São Paulo.

In 1938, Burle Marx was asked to design the landscape setting and roof garden for the new Ministry of Education and Health in the then capital, a building inspired by the design and influence of Le Corbusier. Other commissions, both public and private, quickly followed. By 1950, there was hardly a major building project that was not counting on the hand and eye of Burle Marx to orchestrate the mise-en-scène with exotic, bold designs.

Among the architects with whom he collaborated closely during this period was his friend Reno Levi. Levi shared Burle Marx's passionate interest in tropical plants and traveled with him on his frequent plant-hunting expeditions. It is this close personal and intellectual bond that seems to animate their finest creation, the garden and park created for the house Reno Levi was commissioned to design for industrialist Olivo Gomes.

It was a large order from a sympathetic patron who had actually envisioned the creation of a small new town to surround his estate, although this was not to happen. The gardens of the Gomes Estate were created in two phases, the first coinciding with the completion of the house in 1950. Burle Marx was later asked to extend the grounds by creating a large children's garden that included a swimming pool and an elegant outdoor theater.

Writing in 1972, after Levi's death, Burle Marx recalled earlier conversations with the architect when they had discussed the relationship between architecture and design. With a burning idealism that was frequently defeated, they had seen it as "beauty of form allied to function; interrelation of volumes, forms, colors; aesthetics in relation to social and psychological ends."[1] These somewhat high-flown and vague generalities have taken on a remarkable reality in the Gomes garden.

The commission to design the setting for the large contemporary family house of Olivo Gomes on his estate outside São José dos Campos offered Burle Marx the opportunity to work with a rural setting that he insists is related to the English landscape parks of the eighteenth century carried out by Lancelot Brown and his followers. The patrician encouragement of his patron furthered the analogy, but the results are far removed from a park by Brown or Humphry Repton. It is the scale and bravura that link the Brazilian with the pastoral tradition.

A large, open balcony off the living room, protected by deep eaves, extends toward the formal pool below where the landscape takes up and translates themes laid down by the architecture. The flat countryside has been relieved with lakes and mounds planted with tall grass, giving it the sense of mystery one finds in a Corot landscape. It is, as I have written elsewhere, architecture at home in a rational domain of radically altered nature, conceived in every detail by a master artist gardener.

1. Quoted in Nestor Goulart Reis Filho, "The Architecture of Rino Levi." In *Rino Levi*. Milan: Edizioni di Comunità, 1974.

Woodland Cemetery
Gunnar Asplund

Woodland Cemetery manages to obliterate through the genius of its design the banality of death in the twentieth century. It is a strategy that Carlos Scarpa also employed for the Brion family at San Vito. The landscaped burial ground in Enskede, on the outskirts of Stockholm, was developed between 1917 and 1940 but its origins were more than a hundred years earlier in the opening of Père-Lachaise in Paris in 1804. In people's minds, death underwent a radical change in the eighteenth century when human mortality came to be seen in terms of a new Romantic sensibility.

In Goethe's one-act drama *Elective Affinities*, a discussion takes place about a new cemetery. In the scene, the old and battered gravestones have been taken up and stacked against the church walls. The cleared ground has been smoothed and sown with flowers and grass. The new graves will be placed in this lawn without markers. The dialogue establishes that many people are upset because gravestones are no longer used to mark the place of burial. Goethe's play describes a step toward the landscape or "rural" cemetery in the early nineteenth century, replacing the traditional Christian burial in the churchyard, a right established in the twelfth century.

With the opening of Père-Lachaise the public's attitude toward its deepest beliefs and convictions of life and death shifted, as Richard Etlin has pointed out in *The Architecture of Death*.[1] When the first picturesque cemetery in America began in 1831 with the opening of Mount Auburn, outside Boston, the cemetery park came to express the new emotions and doctrines of immortality.

By the end of the nineteenth century, with the Industrial Revolution in full swing, cities like Stockholm anticipated unprecedented new growth in populations—both of the living and the dead. Later, an international competition for a new cemetery was announced, and Gunnar Asplund, along with his partner Sigurd Lewerentz, won the commission.

Instead of incorporating the fashionable winding drives that provided the circulation system for both park and cemetery on both sides of the Atlantic, from Berlin to Brooklyn, the young partners laid down a network of narrow footpaths through the wooded hillsides, leaving the old forest intact. It was in the forest glens that the graves were placed. An old rock quarry was subtly terraced and planted with trees for additional grave sites. Burial grounds within mature woodlands that had been created earlier at Friedhof Osterholz at Bremen and Waldfriedhof in Munich reflected the new Romantic ideals of man's relationship to nature, in death as in life.

Two chapels were called for. Asplund designed the Woodland Chapel, while Lewerentz carried out the commission for the Chapel of the Resurrection. Asplund's high, pitched, shingled roof, hidden among tall pines, recalls an early Swedish country church. In front of the chapel low earth mounds provide temporary tombs, recalling both the Christ's tomb in Gethsemane and primeval burial mounds of the Nordic past. In the intuitive minimalism and primitive quality of its form, as Stuart Wrede has pointed out in his study of Asplund,[2] the Woodland chapel went beyond the conservative ideas set out by the competition or the popular romantic dreamlands found in the paintings of Arnold Böcklin and Caspar David Friedrich, whose work had been rediscovered the decade before, in 1906. Both artists had been a source of inspiration for cemetery and

1. Richard A. Etlin, *The Architecture of Death: The Transformation of the Cemetery in Eighteenth-Century Paris* (Cambridge: MIT Press, 1980).

2. Stuart Wrede, *The Architecture of Erik Gunnar Asplund* (Cambridge, MIT Press, 1980).

crematorium projects earlier in Germany. Woodland's most moving landscape passage, the Way of the Cross leading up from the entry gate, certainly evokes Böcklin's *Island of the Dead,* but it manages to transcend a merely pictorial or picturesque reference.

The promenade winding quietly up the hill to the main chapel and crematorium by Asplund sustains in the northern landscape an emotional transcendence of great power and comfort. Ceremony is carefully preserved within the democratic real estate of death. On a knoll opposite the chapel, a grove of trees indicates a place on the horizon of special mystery and meditation. The massing of the trees and their trunks echoes in their natural form the sturdy porch of the chapel, sublimely integrating nature with modern architecture. The walk itself is bordered by a wall that somehow heightens the drama of the clean, open parkland.

Asplund had traveled south to Italy and the Mediterranean in 1913–14, just before World War I, and his northern Romantic sensibilities were fired by the surviving fragments of the classical world. In the Way of the Cross, Asplund recalls the Via Sepulcra in Pompeii, lined with its tombs and memorials, a reference that is all the more affecting in the pale Swedish light punctuated by tall, dark pine trees.

Villa Mairea

Alvar Aalto

Coming to terms with nature has not been easy for modern architecture in this century. The landscape setting of modern buildings or the incorporation of a garden into twentieth-century aesthetics has often seemed awkward when viewed within an ideological framework in which form is dictated by those shibboleths of the modern movement of function, material, and technical construction. Functionalists of the 1920s boiled things down even further and claimed that all inspiration should come from practical, empirical needs. But when the vocabulary of the new aesthetics was translated into the realities of landscape design, it did not seem to fit. As Fletcher Steele remarked, most landscape designers fumbled or fled when they attempted to confront the issue. Yet the dilemma had to be resolved if garden art was to play its historic role in the built environment.

The most radical of the Bauhaus architects, who were indifferent to the larger environment of architecture, denied that building was anything more than "social, technical, economic, and psychological organization." Such an arid formula, which left out the irrational element of art and the vagrancy of nature, seemed to cut the ground from beneath the landscape architect who felt much more comfortable working within the traditional, harmonious system offered by the Beaux Arts. It was in this tradition based on classic European precedents that some of the best, if not the most original, garden design was carried out during the first third of the century on both sides of the Atlantic.

Alvar Aalto had been converted to the precepts of the utilitarian, ahistorical arguments of Modernism of the 1920s, yet his architectural work retained deep traditional roots planted in the cultural soil of his native Finland. Le Corbusier's influence was strong in his work, as was that of the Dutch De Stijl school and the Bauhaus. But his biographer, Goran Schildt, has pointed out that beneath this acceptance of technology and functionalism, Aalto's closest, most informing ties were to nature and to the image of harmony he had retained from his childhood in the Finnish woods and vernacular surroundings of rural Finland.

His own solution for incorporating modern architecture into nature would not be the forced geometric system Guevrékian employed at the Villa Noailles, or Le Corbusier's re-creation of Mediterranean fantasies in the suburbs of Paris. Aalto's ideal architectural and landscape image was in the tumbledown Finnish folklore village of Karelia he described as having "grown directly out of natural conditions…its forest architecture pure and simple," where the house has evolved into a symbiotic unity with its surroundings, beginning with a single cell or "dispersed embryonic shacks."

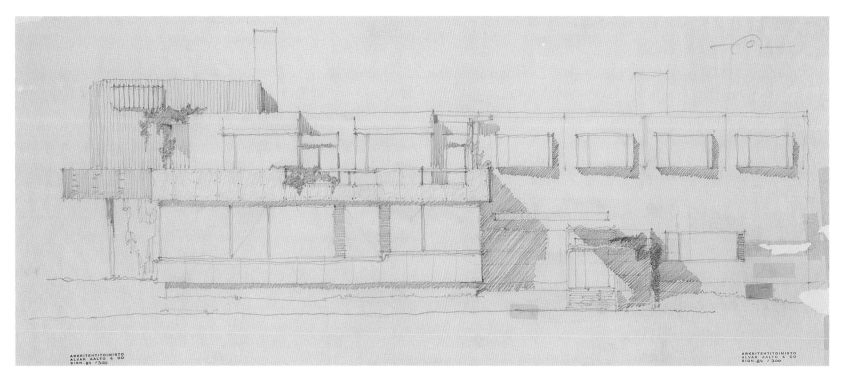

South elevation of Villa Mairea
(Courtesy Alvar Aalto Foundation)

The Villa Mairea was commissioned in 1937 by Harry and Maire Gullichsen to be built in the family compound at Noormarkku, Finland. As he worked quickly from the first cell of inspiration to a recognizable concept, Aalto's earliest sketches were inspired by Frank Lloyd Wright's Fallingwater, which had just appeared in a number of international magazines. But Wright's influence was subsumed as the L-shaped plan with sauna wing and plunge pool emerged. Beyond the sauna was to have been another separate building, long and narrow, to serve as a private art gallery. This idea was abandoned for a large single room in the house for both paintings and books.

The main room is one large, continuous space moved outward through the glass wall opening into the garden, which is enclosed by the house on two sides. In this room and in the open garden space with its free-form pool, Aalto was able to evoke in the modern idiom the vernacular Finnish farmhouse and its close relationship with its surroundings. This feeling is advanced with the sod roof on the sauna, the pergola, and the stone fence with its rustic wooden gate. At the end of the pergola is a primitive fireplace, and at the main entrance of the house slate slabs add a further note of naturalism within the organic conception.

There is also a strong aesthetic connection with Japan, where Aalto had lived for a year before beginning his work at Noormarkku. He admired the Japanese relationship with nature, their "contact…and enjoyment of its constant variation," a quality he wanted to put into the new country house. Both the sauna and the winter garden expressed his interpretation of the Japanese aesthetic.

In 1937, Thomas Church, the California landscape architect, visited Aalto and found himself responding to the relaxed, organic, curvilinear forms in the Finnish architect's buildings, furniture, and garden plans. The plunge pool at the Villa Mairea had not yet been built but its flowing organic form anticipated by a decade Church's famous pool for the Donnell residence at Sonoma. When Church returned to California, his own work reflected Aalto's influence, leading to his El Novillero garden at Sonoma, which Church would design after the war, beginning in 1947.

Alvar Aalto was an important architect and designer of this century. He made no major statements in landscape design, as did Gunnar Asplund or Carlo Scarpa, yet his response to nature and his ability to convey his special affinity for it influenced his and later generations who have labored to find new, flexible living forms for landscape art. The models of artistic harmony he bequeathed are universal.

The Irwin Miller Residence
Dan Kiley

1. "Conversation with Dan Kiley," *Landscape Architecture* (March/April, 1986), p. 52.

2. Ibid.

Dan Kiley's work over more than fifty years is often associated with large commercial and institutional projects. They have ranged from the unbuilt riverfront setting for Saarinen's soaring arch in St. Louis to the terrace gardens of the Oakland Museum and the atrium of the Standard Chartered Bank in the City of London. His geometric lines are sufficiently modernist to go well with the sleek, anonymous glass and steel architecture of I. M. Pei, Harry Wolf, Kevin Roche, and Edward Barnes.

In 1936 Kiley enrolled in the Harvard Graduate School of Design but dropped out after two years. Two of his classmates were Garrett Eckbo and James Rose. As the radicals of the class the three wrote the now celebrated articles published in *Architectural Record* in 1939 and 1940. Kiley's lectures never fail to indict Harvard's dedication to the philosophy of the Beaux Arts school of design, complaining that everything was done by formula and tradition. Yet over the years Kiley has repeatedly paid tribute to André Le Nôtre and the classic French tradition on which the nineteenth- and early-twentieth-century landscape designers relied as much for inspiration as the distant relics of Greece and Rome or the models drawn from the Italian Renaissance. The formula of balance, rhythm, proportion, and spatial hierarchies of the architecture transferred to the landscape had worked as well in Paris as it did in Rome and Florence or on Long Island or in Chicago.

In spite of his protests to the contrary, Kiley's major creations have been in the best Beaux Arts tradition, following the dictates of the architecture in projecting its usually geometric personality into the setting. It is this deft and stylish compatibility with contemporary architecture that creates the ensemble effect, suggesting that the architect himself actually designed his own landscaped setting. This is quite evident in the vast, formal plaza of the United States Air Force Academy in Colorado Springs and in the North Carolina National Bank tower in Tampa, Florida, designed by Harry Wolf. Wolf had adopted a mystical mathematical formula of the fourteenth century as the basis of his proportions, and Kiley took the same formula for the design of the four-and-a-half-acre plaza dominated by a four hundred-foot canal "so that building and plaza become one."[1]

Kiley considers the garden of the Miller residence, completed in 1955, his first modern landscape. Eero Saarinen and Kevin Roche had designed the uncompromisingly modern house. From the large central space, the architecture's rigorously geometric lines extend out into the rectangular site. The movement of the architecture is increased by a raised podium that reaches twenty-five feet beyond the walls of the house as a band of stone terrace and a band of ordered trees. "The house was designed in functional blocks…so I took the same geometry and made rooms outside using trees in groves and allées. And the whole thing becomes a geometry."[2]

No landscape designer in this century has endowed geometry with more poetry and humanity than Dan Kiley. Those worn-out words "proportion," "harmony," "balance," "fitness" seem to take on a new life. Yet his diffident, minimal statements have a gentleness (quite obviously in the Miller grounds) that tames the old aggressions of the Beaux Arts tradition. In many ways he remains that tradition's most persuasive champion and effective interpreter in the late twentieth century.

El Novillero

Thomas Church

In contrast to the Brazilian mountainscape that inspired the drama for Roberto Burle Marx's famed Monteiro Garden, designed in 1947, the same year as El Novillero, Thomas Church had only rocky hills, salt marshes, and live oak groves to draw upon. The domestic scale geared for California living, the needs of the clients, Mr. and Mrs. Dewey Donnell, and the understated setting all entered into Church's calculations.

Church's early career had been devoted to small gardens in and around San Francisco. The seemingly modest demands of the typical garden space of middle-class California did not cause him to lose sight of his conviction that a garden could be a work of art, however. His book *Gardens Are for People*, published in 1955, documented his belief that the garden of the twentieth century must address the realities of American mobility, outdoor family living, irregular plots, and the need for low maintenance. His raised planting beds, wooden screen walls, stone or concrete paving and timber decks introduced a new vocabulary of domestic garden design. Commissions for vacation homes with their informality and the absence of the usual urban restraints allowed him to continue to develop the same vocabulary but with a freedom that was often only an illusion in smaller, urban spaces.

While El Novillero has been singled out by critics as a major accomplishment, two other California gardens, one created in Burlingame, in 1941, and the other for a small beach house at Aptos, dating from 1948, help to enlarge the scope of Church's achievements. The Burlingame garden, especially in the remodeling of the backyard—a space that was classic in its ordinariness—shows Church at his most ingenious and influential. An extended deck and a wide, curving terrace make the garden a functional extension of the house while enlarging the illusion of size.

The garden of the weekend house at Aptos, consists of redwood decking, sand, and ice plant (*Mesebryanthemum edule*) used as ground cover. Clearly, the client's summer living at the beach was not to be dominated by garden work. Yet its simplicity and elegance maintain a relaxed quality appropriate to the West Coast hedonist.

The so-called kidney-shaped swimming pool, which may have been inspired by Alvar Aalto's amoeboid forms, is the centerpiece of El Novillero. Aalto's swimming pool at the Villa Mairea (1938) and the curving lines of Burle Marx's roof garden for the Ministry of Education in Rio, planned in 1936, reflect biomorphic imagery found in the Surrealist painters. As Michael Lancaster has pointed out, Church's design also shows a rare use of Cubist theory in the way the scene constantly shifts simultaneously without a beginning or an end. The form of the pool "cuts across the pattern of concrete and redwood squares, each stressing the rhythm of the other," Lancaster has written. "Line plays against line, form against form, the whole uniting with admirable restraint, into a composition which has its own unique identity, and at the same time belongs essentially to the site."[1]

Trees native to the site push through the spreading redwood deck. Local rocks are incorporated into neo-Zen beds. A sculpted stone rises from the pool itself. There is in the composition a celebration of nature, but of a nature controlled and shaped into art yet utterly in tune with the larger setting and the private satisfaction of the client. The result at El Novillero is an abstract of modern garden design philosophy unsurpassed in the United States. For all of its modernism, its very lack of ideology in the open, California countryside is a part of its enduring charm.

1. In Jellicoe, *Oxford Companion to Gardens*, p. 48.

Brion Cemetery
Carlo Scarpa

In 1959, ten years before he would begin work on the Brion Cemetery, one of the most complex and arresting works of memorial design in the twentieth century, the Italian designer Carlo Scarpa was accused of impersonating an architect in his native city of Venice. He had, the charge read, engaged in the unlawful practice of architecture without a degree and with malice aforethought. In his acquittal, the court ruled that it was every citizen's right to engage in any artistic work he chose without the need of approval of the state.

This ludicrous farce in the life of a major artist is not worth recalling except that it points up an old ambiguity in attempting to categorize neatly the range of achievements resulting from Scarpa's lifelong research "into the balance between form and material; craft and tradition; memory and sensuality," in the words of George Renalli. Later, Scarpa, who enjoyed the nimbus of enigma that surrounded him and his work, refused to present himself as an architect when he was the subject of an exhibition at the XXXIVth Venice Biennale in 1968. He continued to scorn the label to the end of his life. There may have been only a touch of modest irony in his remarks to Spanish students when he said that he should have suggested to the Brion family that they plant a thousand cypress trees instead of building a monument: "A thousand cypresses are a large natural park, and a natural event, in the years ahead, would have produced a better effect than my architecture."

The Brion cemetery is located in the heavily farmed plain of the Veneto near the small village of San Vito d'Altivole at the foot of the Asolo hills that loom in the distance. The approach off the main road is down a country lane defined by old cypress trees, which are found in many Italian graveyards. Some of the trees seem to have been replaced with telephone poles. Scarpa once said that his first idea for the *tombeau Brion* was to approach the place along this avenue and then through the village burial ground itself, filled with "ugly tombs," the path that most visitors still follow. As in so much of Scarpa's work, the dialogue with the past, with collective memory and with its physical presence, is very important and is announced by this calculated introduction passing through layers of a humble past to the new memorial. This willingness to recognize and to incorporate signs of communal history and continuity was as important in the rural landscape of San Vito as in the established, ancient urban patterns of Venice and Verona, where most of his career as designer and architect was spent. He was not complaining when he remarked that he had rarely done anything from scratch. The given context and definition of his work was often old buildings and settings reaching across centuries. But these ancient monuments were called upon to play useful new roles and are not simply restored and renovated. They have been brought to life with more than a transplant or face-lift. The reorganized Castle Vecchio in Verona is now a vital museum of art. The perfectly preserved facade of the Querini Stampalia requires only Scarpa's new bridge from the *campicello* to announce the splendid library, galleries, and garden within.

In the restoration of the early-sixteenth-century Palazzo Querini, the upper floors are reached via a staircase of ancient, worn steps, the old treads partially covered with new slabs of marble. This was not only an act of renewal of the building's fabric in order to preserve its architectural past, but the work of an artist who knew how to orchestrate brilliantly the tension between the old and the new without compromising either. "I renewed the staircase without destroying it," he said in an interview in 1978, "preserving its identity and its history, increasing the tension between the new and the old." Sometimes, his own work is so seamlessly woven into the older fabric that it eludes detection. But Scarpa was not afraid to underline that tension by articulating the intersection of time present and time past in order to make clear the visual and metaphorical logic of the union between the present and the past. He might well have been speaking of his first idea for the Brion cemetery when he said that "the important point of the past is not so much the final solutions but themes that have to be dealt with" in a setting or building heavy with history, even if that history is the old, gloomy, and insignificant burial ground of an obscure community in the province of Trevisio.

If Scarpa has escaped the inhibiting limitations of the professional architect, he is rarely included under the label of landscape or garden designer. Yet the monument commissioned by Onorina Brion for her husband Giuseppe and his family gave Scarpa the opportunity to create one of his most important works as a garden composition. Just as in the nineteenth century American cemeteries like Mount Auburn in Cambridge, Massachusetts, had also served as public parks, he believed that the place of the dead should have the feeling of a garden rather than a collection of rabbit warrens or "piles of shoeboxes stacked up" as in so many modern cities. The very ordinariness of the old existing cemetery with its rustic platitudes on death makes it an unwitting chorus in the drama of Scarpa's achievement.

Given the luxury of the unrestricted commission by the family of a local magnate, "where the rationality of reason might not even exist," he would "show people what the meaning of death, eternity, and the transitory might be....At San Vito I wanted to express the natural meaning of water and fields, of water and earth: water is the source of life."

"A man had died in Italy and his family wanted to honor one who had come up from the people," Scarpa's narrative begins, with the sparse cadence of an ancient myth polished and refined by constant retelling. The family agreed that the new memorial should be a part of its local, social, and rural milieu and so land was acquired at the end of the village adjacent to the community cemetery of San Vito. The size and shape of the plot was determined by the landowner, who insisted on selling an amount of land he felt consistent with the new social standing of the purchaser, Scarpa later complained, contrary to the modest structure he had first envisioned.

The L-shaped area of about two thousand square meters borders the original cemetery on two sides. Scarpa said that the approach was on the axis of the main entryway, through the old cemetery to a high, blank wall dominated by a porch and opening Scarpa called the *propylaeum*. The three steps leading up are slightly off axis, thereby announcing the asymmetry of the plan within. The visitor passes through the wall into a narrow space and, after a moment of confusion, may proceed ahead into the main garden of pool and greensward or turn left down a covered passage, running at right angles, to an entrance with the tomb beyond, on yet another line. A turn to the right, with nothing to direct the way in the dim light, leads to a passage blocked by a glass door. Opposite the entrance porch is an opening composed of two interlocking circles. The layers of ambiguities to be encountered in trying to read the correct itinerary in this entry anticipate the calculated discontinuity that follows. "At every step we are called on to choose, as in life, as in history, as in memory."

The metaphor of the labyrinth has been applied more than once to Scarpa's architecture, but the image of the labyrinth suggests a single, correct deciphering in order to find the ultimate exit. As Manfredo Tafuri has pointed out, Scarpa's work—and it is particularly true of the Brion Cemetery—is not an invitation to discover the true path of a maze. Instead we are to abandon ourselves to the mysteries of experience and to participate in the manifold possibilities of alternative routes and random exploration. Always we must decide.

Several critics have noted the analogy between the open organization and sequences of the complex—pool, tomb, pavilion, lawns—and those of certain Chinese landscape gardens where the visitor could enjoy the variety and movement without any overt direction or guidance.

The sarcophagi of Onorina and Giuseppe Brion are placed asymmetrically in the sunlight at the juncture of the two arms of the site, a recessed, circular space covered by an arch or bridge. Scarpa called it an *arcosolium*, which was a term used for a special niche for the graves of martyrs in the catacombs of Rome. The subtle off-center shift of the tombs modifies the funerary motif, giving the garden narrative an unexpected direction away from the memorial clichés of death. The ostensible focus of the memorial is subordinated to a far more dense and complex scheme than a mere family tomb.

At the opposite end of the open, rectangular space is the cool, shining, and still pool where a pavilion raised on slender, metal legs stands on a small platform in the water. The imperceptibly flowing stream running in a straight line from a source near the tomb perpetuates the Islamic and Christian theme of water's mystical and purifying properties. The lost Garden of Paradise of Genesis and the promised Paradise of the Koran are assimilated in Scarpa's narrow, elegant channel. Almost everyone has commented on the Venetianness of Scarpa's use of water, but it is not only from the dark waters of the canals that he drew his inspiration. It is true that the glass door between the pool and passage opens by sliding down into the water and hints at bulkheads in the canal entries of some Venetian palaces, but the witty mechanisms for opening the door, a parody of physics displayed on the wall overlooking the pool, might have been inspired, as someone suggested, by Paul Klee.

Instead of going through the old cemetery to reach the main space, the strict funerary route for family and mourners is through a gate on the road that leads to the chapel, a concrete cube structure Scarpa placed at a forty-five-degree angle to the pathway, which is isolated by luminous water on all sides except at its two entries. Although private, the chapel can be used by the community and burial space has been set aside for village priests. The reflections of water sent up from the surrounding moat enter into the chapel from vertical windows around the altar, recalling flashes of pale gold light on a medieval ceiling, an alternative reference to the more usual invocation of the refracted light of Venice.

The Brion garden cemetery, threshold to the next life, is a sensual celebration of the human pleasures of light, texture, color, and sound. The concrete is cast in unplaned wooden molds that preserved the wood's graining. The materials and surfaces of the pavements are carefully selected to communicate signs and directions. Footsteps on the hollow steps leading from the chapel up to the tombs give out a subtle echo of a musical scale that shakes the natural and melancholy silence associated with death. Byzantine colored glass and tile are embedded in walls and around openings. Even the stuccoed panels crack and peel as if by design beneath heavy green shrubs.

1. Michael Sorkin, "Scarpa in the Details," *Village Voice*, Dec. 11, 1984.

All other quotations are from Dal Co and Mazzariol, *Carlos Scarpa: The Complete Works*.

Scarpa saw his creation more as a discourse with life than with death, "the only work I go to look at with pleasure," he once declared. He was deeply disturbed by the debased rites of death in the modern world, believing that cemeteries should be places where everyone would be happy to visit, where "the children play and dogs run around....In summer it's lovely, the swallows skim by." He deliberately raised the level of the plot in order to give a view of the flat countryside beyond the wall, which was set at an incline to block the view from outside. The smells and sounds of the surrounding country press in on every side. Climbing vines break up the sharp, geometric edges as in a recently excavated Roman villa ruin. In fact, among the myriad allusions, references, themes, and quotations scholars have deciphered at San Vito, Pompeii, where death also mingles in a strange pagan way with the sensual, has never been mentioned. "It offers…a collection of incidents that proposes to absorb rather than to awe," Michael Sorkin has written, "to animate all the individual acts entailed in graveside visits instead of subsuming them in some unitary symbol of the ineffable: there is no pyramid."[1]

If the Brion family had suddenly decided not to use their walled-in garden as a funerary memorial, it could, borrowing from pagan irony, easily serve as a retreat for entertainments, earthly pleasures, and delectations of a cultivated individual who might, on occasion, invite friends, even lovers, to share his retirement. Both the East of Hadrian's Villa and the Moorish palace of Medina Azahara outside of Cordoba, Spain, come to mind. The East of Scarpa's beloved Japan, where he was to die, is also present. Since Scarpa actually arranged for his own grave within the garden of his patrons, it is not mere fantasy to think that he was also planning San Vito for the long-term preoccupations of his own spirit.

The dust of the Brions in their tombs can easily be ignored in this deliciously Oriental setting where rich materials, textures, and colors seduce the eye. The curve of the arch above the sarcophagi of the Brions is faced with gilt and enameled tiles.

The pavilion floating on the pool could be a place to meet a lover on a moonlit night. Is this what the artist had in mind when he included the ghostly sketch of a nude woman seated in the pavilion in one of his drawings? The critic Michael Sorkin has even detected telltale wine stains on some of the sheets.

Given Scarpa's receptive imagination capable of responding to art throughout history, it is probably misleading to attempt to isolate and identify all of the influences hidden in his work. It would be difficult to name another artist whose landscape design absorbs so many memories in organization and details. Piero della Francesca, Mondrian, Klee, Frank Lloyd Wright, Josef Hoffmann, the Katsura Imperial Villa, a miniature of Babur's harem garden at Agra, Matisse, are only fragments of memory, names in capricious association until translated into a coherent discourse as in a poem or musical composition. In the disjunctive logic that Scarpa mastered at Brion with its wit, surprises, and intelligence, he was able to "wed speech and silence, play and serenity, the need for utterance and…the wavering, troubled thought."

San Cristobal
Luis Barragán

"Any architecture that does not express serenity is a mistake," the landscape architect Luis Barragán declared, decrying the "intemperate use of enormous glass windows" in contemporary houses. Richard Neutra's "generous opening to health agents," his euphemism for his picture windows, must have sounded like a regulation promulgated by a municipal sanitation commission to the cultivated, Latin imagination of the Mexican. Barragán saw a house and its garden as a refuge, an ancient tradition of walled privacy that ran from Mexico to Islamic Spain of the twelfth century and on into the dim garden mythology of the Middle East. Like Wright's recollections of growing up on a Wisconsin farm, Barragán's childhood memories of a rustic family life on a ranch near the village of Mazamitla remained a protean source of inspiration throughout his life. An element of nostalgia and memoir are never far below the surface of his work.

An engineer by training, Barragán had discovered the contemporary writings of Ferdinand Bac. Bac's belief in "an art which builds upon all our nostalgic reminiscences of places where we would like to have set up our tent and remain, uplifted by Beauty and strengthened by Simplicity" struck an emotional chord. Bac's bold use of color in his neo-Mediterranean gardens along the French Riviera may have also influenced Barragán's own startling palette of pinks, yellows, and magentas used to animate his austere architecture. Strong color on flat wall planes is a key element in the austere composition of his gardens and houses, as are the sober and monumental forms. Paint is applied to the architectural garden elements as to a stage set, giving his work a sense of theater, as Emilio Ambasz has observed, a property that the Modern movement has neglected or ignored altogether. Barragán's use of color is also derived from the abstract color field proposed by contemporary painters of his generation.

The Mexican came late to landscape architecture, and his garden language is that of a poet retelling a myth in inexhaustible variations. His most complex creation (and, sadly, the only project that is still maintained in its original condition) is the estate of San Cristobal in the suburbs of Mexico City, dating from 1967–1969. The complex consists of a house, swimming pool, horse pool, and stable where thoroughbreds are raised and trained. The center of action is the stable near the house and the horses that live and are groomed there occupy a surreal theater set. Not since the great horse water tank at Marly was built in the late seventeenth century to terminate the water displays at Louis XIV's garden retreat have equine ablutions been elevated to such high art. In the house, with its private plaza, in the trough projection feeding water into the horse pool, and in the paddock where grooms are choreographed in their movements to care for their charges, the analogue of Barragán's childhood village is made manifest in the ritual of his stunning creation. His recollection of similar childhood scenes serves as the myth in which the work at San Cristobal is embedded. San Cristobal is also a rare demonstration of the architect, like the poet, turning to private reveries and elusive memory as a source of inspiration.

It was a *pueblo* with hills, formed by houses with tile roofs and immense eaves to shield passersby from the heavy rains in the area. Even the earth color was interesting because it was red earth. In this village, the water distribution system consisted of great gutted logs, in the form of troughs, which ran on a support structure of tree forks, five meters above the roofs. This aqueduct crossed over the town, reaching the patios, where there were great stone fountains to receive the water. The patios housed the stables, with cows and chickens, all together. Outside, in the street, there were iron rings to tie the horses. The channeled logs, covered with moss, dripped water all over town, of course. It gave this village the ambiance of a fairy tale.[1]

1. Racine et al., p. 112.

All other quotations are from Ambasz, *The Architecture of Luis Barragán.*

The Kennedy Memorial at Runnymede

Sir Geoffrey Jellicoe

When the British government decided to create a memorial to John F. Kennedy, it turned to Geoffrey Jellicoe, whose lifelong interest in landscape design provided a unique intellectual and aesthetic perspective for such an important commission. Trained as an architect, Jellicoe decided in his early twenties to make an extensive study of Italian gardens with J. C. Shepherd, which led to their book *Italian Gardens of the Renaissance,* published in 1925. It was illustrated with elegant Beaux Arts elevations and plans in the high style of that pictorial tradition, becoming a classic on the subject.

At the outset, the committee named to oversee the commission decided that the memorial was to appeal to the visitor's intellect rather than the eye to perpetuate the memory of the slain American president, a memory that was overwhelmingly wrought with emotion. In 1964, when the commission was initiated, the aura of myth on an Alexandrian scale had already overtaken the event and the personality of the president, blocking any measured judgement on their place in history. Both the government's gesture and the artist's response must be seen in the context of this twentieth-century attempt to address a tragedy without "the divine for which all men long" (in words from the *Odyssey*) to cushion and explain inexplicable events.

Over the decades, and not always with visual success, Jellicoe had attempted to build intellectual content into his work by thinking about landscape design in allegorical, symbolic terms, a rare preoccupation in this century. From his investigations into the past he was well aware that the classic memorial for a murdered hero, such as a monumental statue, a memorial arch, or a broken column, was a gesture no longer possible in the modern world. The committee's early selection of the site and its charge that the only architectural feature was to be a simple podium helped to resist any pictorial temptations. The tragic event the memorial was called upon to mark inspired the sixty-five-year-old artist to search for a design that would somehow lift the drama of Kennedy's death at the height of his power above "the gentle and modest English countryside."[1]

That specific countryside Jellicoe speaks of is an acre of land halfway up the side of a hill overlooking Runnymede, where in 1266 the first charter of individual freedom was signed. This piece of historic real estate, primitive meadowland looking out over the level fields where the barons' upper hand of force was translated into a cornerstone of human rights, was to be the central visual monument. An adjoining strip of land belonging to the National Trust was dedicated to provide access to the acre plot.

1. Jellicoe, *Guelph Lectures on Landscape Design*, p. 86.

All other quotations are from Jellicoe, *Studies in Landscape Design*.

In the beginning, the basic idea for the landscape composition was decided upon. Everything would follow from this concept, which was to be what the Greeks called "the universals" according to Jellicoe's recollection. "It should not…be recognizably of any style of architecture, creed, or personal taste of the designer, who should be anonymous." Jellicoe's own description of the stages that followed cannot be adequately paraphrased. It is a unique document detailing the evolution of landscape design in the twentieth century. Even in its telling, he cannot resist the analogy to John Bunyan's *Pilgrim's Progress* as a precedent for his own account, like Bunyan, explaining and rationalizing an allegory in the course of telling the story. Here is Jellicoe's sketch of the evolution of the program guiding the design:

The decision that the landscape, and only the landscape, was the memorial. Any stone or descriptive tablet would be explanatory only.

Because the memorial stood for harmony between two nations, there should appear to be no boundaries between the territories. This led to the concealment of the necessary fences between adjoining properties, and the adoption of the ha-ha, or sunk fence.

The recognition that the genius loci depended first upon the green, undisturbed slopes, and thereafter on the nature of the trees and hedgerows already existing on the site, into which the new designs would need to be woven.

The approach could only be up through the woods, and it seemed logical that the dedication be placed at the head of the path and the entrance to the field. One of the features of the site is the view and the logical step was to select the best viewpoint for a contemplative seat or seats. This should be as far as possible across the field, since the panorama would be seen here at its best. With these factors it was not difficult to choose the terrain where the path across the field could run parallel with the slopes and where existing thorn trees could provide shade for the seats. The stone would be shaded by mixed woodland trees. The seats would dig into the hillside.

We now therefore have a composition of two major and apparently equal elements, the stone and the seats. This is technically known as a "duality of interest." The unifying element must be the landscape itself.

Since we have no architectural style to help us, whether historic or modern, Western or Eastern, we must evolve an art that is based on those proportions which have proved themselves to be significant and agreeable to the human race at all times and in all places.

Jellicoe then explains the allegory of the woodland path, the stone, and the formal path and seats. The small Portuguese setts or paving stones, used for random steps in the woods and numbering over fifty thousand "represent the multitudes for whom Kennedy stood as a champion of freedom." They were scattered like a crowd attending an English football match.

The wood through which the path gropes its way upwards is symbolic of the virility and mystery of nature as a life force. The wood is left in its natural state to be dark and forbidding to recall the "dark wood" of Dante.

The allegory of the white stone marker is that of a catafalque being carried on the shoulders of the hero's followers. The seats, inspired by Henry Moore's *King and Queen* installed in the landscape at Moore's estate, represent the public image of the president at the upper level and that of his consort in the secondary position.

Fitting this precise, freighted concept into the quotidian rustic landscape was intended to evoke a primitive scene crowned by a Greek temple in the distance. It was this idea of a temple that dictated the scale as "aloof and heroic."

Of the tens of thousands of people who visit the memorial each year, few if any will have a clue to the sophisticated, cerebral concept that underpins the design. Yet each has come as a pilgrim to pay homage to a fallen hero. In this gesture all are united in an ancient undertaking for which the artist has prepared the shrine, a shrine that is as moving in its indestructible, universal language as anything that an age without convictions can hope to create.

Stonypath

Ian Hamilton Finlay

1. Gintz, p. 112.

A biographical note on the eighteenth-century literary gardener William Shenstone in *The Oxford Companion to Gardens* begins "English poet and landscape theorist, and creator of his own much admired garden." If Scottish were substituted for English, we would have the opening line for a biographical entry on one of the remarkable figures in modern gardening. Shenstone and, of course, Alexander Pope, as poets working in the landscape, would be closer in spirit to Finlay than any gardener/artist since the eighteenth century.

Ian Hamilton Finlay started his professional life as a short-story writer and poet of the "concrete" persuasion before he settled in the southern uplands of Lanarkshire, Scotland, in 1966. There he took up residence in a dilapidated croft on a desolate stretch of countryside, where he wrote and corresponded with a wide circle of friends as well as the merely curious while building model boats and airplanes as a hobby. In this poetic retreat, over the next two decades Finlay gradually transformed the unpromising compound into a modern literary garden, converting old sheds and farm buildings into "temples" with a few touches of classical elements dedicated to Apollo, Philemon, and Bacchus. Topographical features became the Roman Garden, the Temple Pool, and, to make his identity with the English pastoral tradition clear, a grotto dedicated to Dido and Aeneas. The facade of a stone cottage was made into the Temple of Apollo by affixing four Corinthian pilasters and painting the words "HIS MVSIC—HIS MISSILES—HIS MVSES." Like Pope's garden at Twickenham, "it was [in the words of Horace Walpole] a singular effort of art and taste to impress so much variety and scenery on a spot of five acres."

As Claude Gintz has pointed out in "Neoclassical Rearmament," his essay on Finlay, Pope's garden was more than a poet's retreat for meditation, becoming in its celebration of antique Roman virtues and rustic simplicity a commentary and counterattack on the political and cultural corruption that had spread throughout English society, summed up in his "Epistle to Lord Burlington." Stonypath, renamed Little Sparta in 1978 after a tax war with the regional council government, became an even more obvious redoubt for a "political and cultural offensive which the poet directs against the wider world."[1] From this base, Finlay has kept up his polemical attacks not only in the garden itself, but in a steady barrage of publicity, exhibitions, and letters to the growing list of correspondents scattered throughout the world.

Finlay has an uncanny, poetic way of introducing symbols and ideas into the garden in the form of quotations and symbolic objects, a technique that Shenstone perfected at his own garden The Leasowes, in Warwickshire, England, during the 1740s and 50s. The message can be subtle and elegiac, as in the miniature stone aircraft carrier commemorating the Battle of Midway with the sleek symbol of naval destruction. In this gesture and in the sculpture *Nuclear Sail*, which is in fact the conning tower of a nuclear submarine, Finlay makes clear that he is no Romantic or nationalist zealot, but a revolutionary who uses the garden as a means of delivering his unsettling critique of contemporary society. In the Temple of Apollo, Finlay has installed a small museum where, among other brutally witty objects, there is a reproduction of Bernini's *God of Music* holding a hand grenade. Beside the Temple Pool, for example, there are the familiar initials "AD" engraved on a stone slab to recall not only the sacrifice of the Christian God but more specifically to remind us of an earlier landscape, the watercolor *The Great Piece of Turf* by Albrecht Dürer, who signed the work with his initials. Who can bear to recall that beautiful tribute to nature when confronted with the desolation of the modern environment? Finlay's poetic language resonates with subtle allusions as in a symbolic watercan decorated with a tricolor cockade, referring to the faith the French revolutionaries had in the regenerative, life-giving power of spilled blood—"watering the tree of Liberty with the blood of Tyrants." It also alludes to the word *arrosoir*, the French word for watering can, a machine gun, and the day in the revolutionary calendar on which Robespierre was guillotined.

During his war with the Scottish tax authorities called "The Battle of Little Sparta," those who supported Finlay (in what some took to be nothing more than a rustic Happening) received a medal from the poet carrying the word *Terror* on one side with an image of the guillotine. On the reverse *Virtue* was illustrated with a pair of classical columns. The words were apt, for Finlay has often used the emblems and maxims of the French Revolution, recalling Saint-Just, Robespierre, and others, who, in the name of Roman ideals and Virtue, and of the simple pastoral life celebrated by Rousseau, led civilization into a series of violent cycles of tyranny and destruction that continue to the present day. The founders of the modern world, in other words, were unwilling to look at the other side of the coin of Virtue. As Jean Starobinski wrote in his study of the symbols of the French Revolution *The Emblems of Reason*, "Reason, conscious of its powers, could unify mankind in the light of the good and the clarity of the intellect. It believed that it could convert everything into light." Against this neoclassical illusion of the dialectics of progress, of secularism and commercialization, Finlay has made his attacks, marshaling his arguments in gardens beyond Stonypath/Little Sparta in Vienna, Florence, San Diego, and the Netherlands.

In 1989 the president of the Republic of France was to have opened a creation by the Scottish gardener in a new permanent garden at Versailles commissioned to commemorate the French Revolution. The site itself was the space once occupied by the demolished l'Hotel de l'Assemblée, which was where the king had summoned the Estates General in 1789 as well as the birthplace of the Revolution. The Ministry of Culture abruptly canceled the project when a small cabal, as a political strategy, spread the slander on the eve of a national election in France that Finlay was anti-Semitic and a proto-Nazi. Even his innocent letters to Albert Speer regarding Speer's garden making while a prisoner were used to spread the canard.

The canceled garden of Versailles has already become something of a cultural and political myth, a condition few other garden projects have achieved in this century. Its title, *"Un Jardin Revolutionnaire,"* was another example of Finlay's ability to make his point with unexpected verbal gestures. In fact, behind the gates was to have been a serene city park in which the grass lawn dominating the center filled exactly the area of the seating used by the deputies. On unworked blocks of stone, a sentence from Michelet's *History of the French Revolution* was to have summed up the spirit of the *Droits de l'Homme*. Between the stones would have been planted wild cherry trees to allegorize the two main aspects of the Revolution—the titanic and the pastoral.

No artist in this century has so forthrightly dared to reclaim the role of gardener-philosopher and to express in garden design his skepticism of the dominant cultural values of the West, his belief in the power of truth and in reason and dialogue as properties of our artistic and political culture, the traditional language of the literary garden. At Stonypath, Finlay asks the visitor to decipher the messages he has hidden along paths and in corners as fragments of their own culture now obliterated by the modern world. Not since the eighteenth century has a poet-gardener attempted to translate his message in the medium of nature.

Paley Park

Zion and Breen and Associates

Even though it is called a park, this small, urban space one hundred feet deep and the width of two New York town houses could be called a public garden just as well, since size is usually a distinguishing element. It is also a water theater, with a waterfall curtain descending across the entire rear wall, drawing visitors into the shaded enclosure by its sparkle and rhythmic sound.

In its minimalist restraint and disdain for any hint of worn-out systems of aesthetics, Paley Park continues to respond to the needs of people caught in the everyday tensions of urban life. Its very order, form, and unity of design are part and parcel of its function as a temporary stopover to refuel jaded nerves battered by the city.

The layout was dictated by the removal of two old town houses that had served most recently as the Stork Club and the decision by the donor, William Paley, to make a garden, a quiet oasis in memory of his father. Since the space for visitors was at a premium, nothing was allowed to intrude except the small, scattered shade trees.

The aesthetics that Robert Zion had assimilated in the Bauhausian atmosphere of the Harvard Graduate School of Design, headed by Walter Gropius, when he entered in 1947, enabled him deftly to employ contemporary principles already shaping architecture, sculpture, and painting but all too often forgotten when it came to gardens and parks. The function of the modern urban park is to provide an island for a brief physical restoration and at the same time substitute an idealized surrounding as a relief from the constant visual assault of city squalor. Paley Park unifies these two purposes, giving a new coinage to the debased meaning of "functional design." Here purpose is subordinated to the all-pervasive quality of peace and quiet in an unlikely place.

Sculpture Garden, Museum of Modern Art

Philip Johnson

1. Kassler, p. 58.

A garden seems an obvious setting for large and important pieces of sculpture. The changes of natural light, the juxtaposition of stone, bronze, or lead with the green texture of bushes and the vertical lines of tree trunks add something to the sensuous pleasure of sculpture that is missing in the purely architectural space of a gallery.

In the early sixteenth century, when Italians began to discover large quantities of ancient marbles during the excavations for their new palaces and villas or in nearby Roman ruins, sheer quantity made it impossible to accommodate these treasures in their houses, so they overflowed outdoors to terraces, arbors, and other garden settings. The sculpture, old or newly commissioned, was worked into the garden's design as an integral element. It was an approach that had little or nothing to do with the siting of contemporary sculpture in an outdoor space using nature as an outdoor art gallery. The modern sculpture garden is uniquely a phenomenon of this century.

The original garden of the Museum of Modern Art was created in 1955. At that time rectilinear space could be seen and easily reached through the museum's main entry hall and announced to the visitor that it was a gallery space equal to those within the building itself. Architecture, sculpture, trees, plants, and water were made into an inviting, sympathetic environment. The small café and open terrace, slightly raised, contributed to a surprisingly casual ambiance. The high gray brick walls served as a perfect foil for the silhouettes of both trees and sculpture in any season. By design or more probably by chance, shadows could also play seductively on these blank walls.

By grouping the trees in clusters of single species—cryptomeria, birch, European hornbeam, and weeping beech—as Elizabeth Kassler has observed, the severity of the geometry is greatly mitigated, creating "a fine reciprocity between formality and freedom."[1]

In 1964, Johnson carried out major additions to the east of the original space, and further changes were made when the central galleries were completely rebuilt to new designs. The space paralleling the garden became the main circulation route for the museum, altering the visitors' passing relationship and making it somehow also more passive as they now move up and down on escalators, looking through sealed glass walls. The very generosity of the high-priced Manhattan real estate as a setting for major works of sculpture is breathtaking and for all the changes, the sculpture garden as an exhibition gallery remains a maturing and appealing model without serious challenge from others that have followed.

Fallingwater
Frank Lloyd Wright

1. Creese, p. 249.

2. Frank Lloyd Wright, *An Autobiography* (New York: Horizon Press, 1976), p. 370.

3. ——. "Taliesin," *Liberty* (March 1929): 22.

4. Ibid.

5. Kaufmann, Introduction, p. 6.

6. Ibid., p. 104.

7. Ibid., p. 126.

Main floor plan of Fallingwater
(L. D. Astorino & Associates, Ltd.)

Frank Lloyd Wright did not consider landscape architecture among his soaring talents but no architect in this century responded more deeply to nature and to the landscape. He was, as Walter Creese has said, far more prolific and committed to inventive architectural solutions when he was working directly with nature in the country or suburbs, even though some of his most brilliant designs are in the heart of the city.

Wright's lyric recollection of Spring Valley, Wisconsin, in *An Autobiography* leaves no doubt how much this modest farm landscape where he was born and where he would build Taliesin meant to him psychologically and aesthetically throughout his life. He was, like Thomas Jefferson, brought up and marked by a personal "sea view" of the landscape drawn from early experience, and in Creese's words, "its ever-shifting, mysterious and rejuvenating character."[1] Both Jefferson and Wright were drawn into the protective arms of nature, and found that architecture and landscape were means of expressing this special affinity. "There must be some kind of house," Wright wrote of the family farm in Wisconsin, "that would belong to that hill as trees and hedges did; as grandfather and mother had, in their sense of it all."[2] Before he was twenty Jefferson had also determined that a house uniquely designed in his image must crown the hill he called Monticello that loomed up a mile to the west of Sladwell, his birthplace.

In his memoir of his father's house, Fallingwater, Edgar Kaufmann, Jr., illustrated the introduction with a Japanese wood print by Hokusai showing a farmhouse on a knoll and a waterfall plunging down beside it. This Oriental scene is a perfect rebus for the subject of the book but also serves to remind us of Wright's own life-long interest in Japan and the earthbound organic life that underpinned the aesthetic of culture. "Ever since I discovered the print, Japan has appealed to me as the most romantic, artistic country on earth. Japanese art, I found, really did have organic character, was nearer to the earth and a more indigenous product of native conditions of life and work, therefore more modern as I saw it, than any European civilization alive or dead."[3] Wright was entranced by the unity of building and landscape, the shining brow on the hill announcing peace and balance with nature. Long before Christopher Tunnard and others were proposing that Japan offered a fresh inspiration to renew the exhausted vision of American landscape architecture, Wright had turned there to discover that "beneficent inner quiet our art so needs."[4]

In 1934, Edgar Kaufmann, then a young artist studying in New York, read Wright's autobiography and sensed that the architect filled in certain gaps missing in his own life, which he felt to be now adrift after his return from Europe. After joining the Taliesin Fellowship in Wisconsin, Kaufmann introduced the architect to his father, a businessman in Pittsburgh. The two men hit it off and, in a short time, Wright found himself a houseguest of the senior Kaufmanns and was taken to their rugged forest retreat overlooking Bear Run Falls in southern Pennsylvania.

The property had originally served as an employees' retreat for the family department store and had been upgraded to a rustic summer camp for the Kaufmanns some ten years before Wright arrived on the scene. This background is significant, for it connects Fallingwater to the older American landscape tradition among the rich of establishing elegant "camps" in the wilderness of the Catskills and Adirondacks among picturesque, romantic settings. As Mark Girouard has pointed out, these "cottage-camps" had to "cater to a life 'ostensibly dominated by nature and its ways' while at the same time maintaining a high standard of living and comfort within."[5] Above all, the architecture must exercise the utmost tact so as to leave "the woods woodsy, seeming a part of their natural surrounding" as a contemporary magazine advised. In many ways the formula was as precise as the design conventions for a Japanese teahouse.

When Edgar Kaufmann, Sr., led Wright down some old stone steps to a flat rock at the base of the falls, the architect was captivated by the scenery and the dramatic torrents of water pouring over the ledge above. Wright saw the opportunity to design a house for this American "desert" in the spirit of Thoreau, where nature is viewed as a lost ideal rather than as something to be cultivated and improved. Nature was now to be seen as a source of psychic rejuvenation and reverence, following the philosophy of J.-J. Rousseau. "What we wanted at Fallingwater," the younger Kaufmann has written, "was neither lordly stateliness nor a mimicry of frontier hardiness, but a good place for city people to renew themselves in nature."[6] The creation of the great national parks, beginning in the mid-nineteenth century with its growing urban congestion, was very much a reflection of this romantic faith that Wright would now interpret for his worldly new clients in this venerable American forest.

The planning and disposition of the house was not to disturb the setting. There was to be no garden beyond what nature itself provided. No trees were to be cut beyond those that made way for the building itself. Any new planting was to blend into the natural surroundings. A large tree near the entrance was preserved by casting a structural beam with a bend in it. Open terraces were provided for sleeping and for enjoying the views.

For nearly forty years, Wright had perfected his craft and his design skills to create architecture that would accommodate its natural surroundings, keeping "the setting unscathed." And as Edgar, Jr., points out, "every room in the house is continued outside, reaching freely into nature without infringement." The cantilevered terraces of Fallingwater may be luxuries, but they also serve as elegant bridges to integrate art into nature, the "real protagonist of Wright's design." The spirit of the Beaux Arts thrust of the architecture was internalized and balanced, and held in check like a Mozart concerto, to conform to nature's embracing orchestration. Below the house and downstream, the terraces and parapets seem to take charge of the monumental rock ledges, "echoing, completing and ordering them....Water and building repeatedly conjoin beginning with the balcony of the living room over the falls....Running water spouts out cheerfully at the entry way and again pours down into a tranquil plunge pool at the east end of the house....The sound of running water permeates the air of Fallingwater."[7]

Wright's work instantly communicates its ease and sympathy with its setting. He has looked at nature with his mind and his heart. He has rejected the alienation one often feels in the work of Le Corbusier, opting for a language of accommodation learned out of experience and knowledge, spoken with a native genius all his own.

Le Parc de la Villette
Bernard Tschumi

All quotations are from Bernard Tschumi, *Cine-gramme Folie: Le Parc de la Villette.*

"Built exclusively for delight, gardens are like the earliest experiments in that part of architecture that is so difficult to express with words or drawings: pleasure and eroticism. Whether 'romantic' or 'classic,' gardens merge the sensual pleasure of space with the pleasure of reason, in the most useless manner."

Bernard Tschumi is an architect of ideas whose reflection on the analogue of the conceptual stage of architecture to the emotional experience of the pleasure garden helps to penetrate the most complex public garden/park created in this century. La Villette is located on a large, denatured piece of ground at the edge of northeastern Paris. The debased, fragmented condition of the proposed park in the late twentieth century at that physical and metaphorical junction between the city and the *banlieues* resembled, in the language of Victor Hugo, the violent, unpredictable confrontation between the land and the sea or as now traffic swirls on the turbulent *périphérie* around the fringes of the space.

The demoralized condition of the 125 acres that the French government decided to transform into an "urban park of the twenty-first century" in 1983 was just the kind of loaded terrain to stimulate the highly intellectual sensibility of the Swiss-born architect. His response to the terms of the design competition organized by the government was both subtle and original, engaging by reference in his strategy the ideas of some of the leading writers and intellectuals of the century. Foucault, Blanchot, Derrida, and Barthes were called upon to supply the literary text for La Villette in much the same way as the texts of classical poets were often deployed by gardeners and architects in eighteenth-century

England. But Tschumi's understanding of the literature of his time and its relevance to the urban condition in the late twentieth century distinguishes, of course, his use of history, art, and philosophy from any comparison with Pope and Kent and other Augustan worthies who drew upon remote, romantic sources to support them in the landscape revolution of their day. Nostalgia and sentiment, which are unacknowledged components of post-Modern fashion, are not a part of Tschumi's sensibility, even though he is capable of accommodating the past, even of a slaughterhouse, without contradicting his contemporary aesthetics.

The site had originally been just outside the eighteenth-century boundaries of Paris and had been occupied by the city's central abattoir well into the twentieth century. The stench and the sounds of animals in death throes consigned the quarter to the lowest standard of degraded living, reserved for the workers and their families. Its noisome presence was a condition that the bourgeois of Paris did not want to confront, going out of their way to avoid it when traveling north through the city to their country estates. Even after most of the surviving nineteenth-century iron structures were torn down, an attempt was made to build housing blocks on the site, but this partially completed scheme was abandoned not long before the government decided that culture might be injected in heavy doses as a sounder strategy both to utilize the space and to rejuvenate the working-class district.

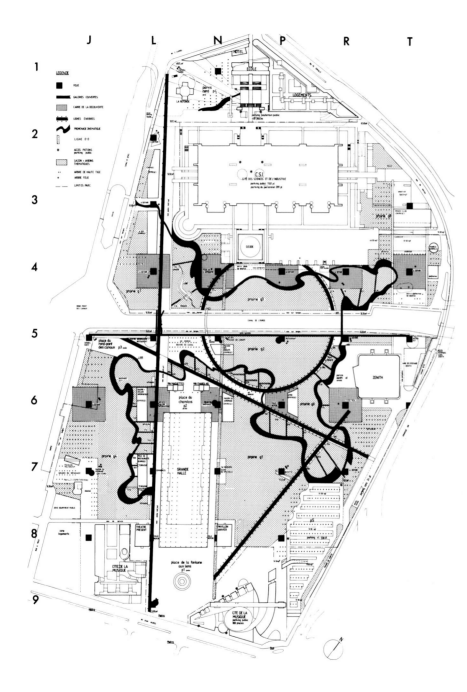

The program for the competition envisioned a complex development of cultural and entertainment facilities for open-air theaters, restaurants, art studios, galleries, and music workshops, and facilities for film, video, and computer art. A science museum already occupied brutal new concrete behemoths and a surviving *halle* from the original *Marche aux Bestaux* was slated to be turned into a rock concert hall and exhibition space. By the time of the competition, it was emphatically not "virgin land," as the architect has written. All agreed that future programs and uses of the park would remain unknown because of changing, unpredictable budgets, priorities, and institutional politics. The job for the architect and park designer was "to find an organizing structure that would negate the simplistic assumption of a causal relationship between a program and the resulting architecture. The Utopia of present or future unity through architectural intervention was out of the question." In every sense, it was to be an existential urban park on a major scale.

Tschumi resisted the traditional strategies of urban landscape design, beginning with an inspired composition, the contextual completion of an already existing design, or, as in American parks, representing a reconstruction of nature in the romantic gesture of Olmsted and his followers. Believing that gardens have often anticipated the history of cities while at the same time combining the garden's "sensual pleasures of space with the pleasure of reason," Tschumi accepted the unpredictability of the urban condition and the need to be open to infinite possibilities through combination and substitution—any design tendency toward a hierarchy of focus and organization was resisted.

Tschumi's plan for Parc de la Villette
(Bernard Tschumi Architects)

The architect imposed several grids on the site but a serial grid on a coordinate system at 120-meter intervals was selected to establish a strong territorial image over an ill-defined terrain. The grid's regularity gives the visitor a clear but minimal orientation with a ten- by ten- by ten-meter cube marking the intersections of the imaginary grid. In the mind of the architect, the overall space of the Parc de la Villette might be imagined as one vast building, discontinuous but still a single structure "overlapping in certain areas with the city and existing suburbs." It could not be further from Olmsted's dictum that "in the park, the city is not supposed to exist." The garden/park is no longer a passive background, a place for spiritual repose.

The grid of the park is related to a larger coordinate linking the north-south pedestrian walk running between the two public gates and subway stations and intersecting with an east-west coordinate running along the bank of the ancient Canal de l'Ourcq. This walk divides the park and links the city with the suburbs beyond.

Because the individual red steel cubes, or *folies*, as Tschumi calls the marking points or structures, have become a powerful symbol for La Villette in their sculptural variety and glistening red surfaces, sight of the intelligence behind the larger plan has been lost. Their abstract forms give new meaning to the disjunction and dissociation of the older architecture scattered over the site. While the architect has claimed that his intervention through the placing of the *folies* on a formal grid pattern does not refer to a typology or historical ideal, there is more than a hint of the Cartesian order that has underlined French garden and urban design for years.

The scale of La Villette is overwhelming and can be depressing, as a French park of the seventeenth century can be a melancholy experience when empty. But the lack of symmetry and hierarchy that can encourage aimlessness has been replaced with a meandering promenade relating sequentially to the various parts of the park. Since it is not yet completed, it is difficult to evaluate. Tschumi has described it as a "montage of sequences and frames conceived as spaces for the intervention of artists, landscape designers, architects, and philosophers. A film strip in which the soundtrack corresponds to the pedestrian path and the image track to the successive frames of specific gardens aimed at such activities as bathing, picnicking, roller skating as well as the staging of 'natural planting' or conceptual gardens." This carefully orchestrated circuit seems to contradict the existential philosophy that claims resolute neutrality for the architect's comprehensive intervention.

Tschumi accepts as a fact that the terms "park" and "garden" (like "architecture," "science," or "literature") have lost their conventional, universal meaning in the sense of an absolute or an ideal—"Not the *hortus conclusus* and not the replica of Nature," they are words that have become unstable, their meaning always eluding us in their dynamic transformation into a multiplicity of meanings. Where we once believed we saw reflected an ideal image of Nature or pristine Utopian miniature world, we are asked to confront the city as it exists and to serve the needs of a less than Utopian citizenry who will themselves supply the programs of their urban culture. "To create false hills hiding the périphérique ignores the power of the urban reality." Tschumi's sensibility has revived the pleasure of spaces for events not yet invented or imagined. His structure of reason is built on a grid of *folies*, for he knows, as Goya reminded us, that "the sleep of Reason produces madness."

The Isamu Noguchi Museum Garden

Isamu Noguchi

All quotations are from Noguchi, *The Isamu Noguchi Museum Garden.*

The image of Isamu Noguchi's sculpture is so powerful that his work as a designer of landscapes has largely been overlooked. Yet his sensitivity to "landscape," both in individual works of sculpture that refer to the contours of idealized space in their composition and in their intended physical placement within a larger landscape setting, has been obvious throughout his long career. A small black granite sculpture named *This Place*, which stood for years in his garden in Japan, was called by Noguchi "a landscape in a landscape." Nature's eventual bonding with the sculpture when weeds in the garden grew up in the interstices of the stone literally turned the work into a miniature garden.

The monumental stone that would eventually become *Mono Taro* was found on the island of Shodoshima and seemed itself to be a piece of natural sculpture *in situ*, yet according to the artists its ultimate transformation into a work of art was inspired by the sculpted hill and landscape at the Storm King Art center at Mountainville, New York. The unity between the white sculpture and its surroundings of green lawn and background trees imposes an ideal order by means of subtle positioning of the carved stone.

Another example of the sculptor's fusion of sculpture with his garden design is the Sunken Garden of the Beinecke Library at Yale University, where the entire garden space, forty by fifty feet, has been created as a single piece of marble sculpture. Except for the fact that no weed will ever intrude here, this singular garden is an enlargement of the concept of *This Place* in the artist's own Japanese garden. Here, on a full scale dictated by the architect, Gordon Bunshaft, Noguchi was allowed to explore that obsessive problem of space as it relates both to sculpture and to landscape design.

Noguchi has written that his earliest efforts to investigate this problem came in 1935, when he was asked by Martha Graham to design dance sets for her company. The illusions called for in the theater, the symbolism that could be employed, the limitations in which to work, the impermanence of the medium, allowed the artist an opportunity for unprecedented experiment. Experiment and search, breaking new ground, he said many times, was at the heart of his work as an artist. Whether he recognized it or not, Noguchi was continuing an old Western tradition reaching back to the early Italian Renaissance, as well as the later French and English courts, in which artists moved freely between dance, theater, and garden design. There is evidence that similar design experience also occurred in early Japan. The connection between religious dance rituals and the historical evolution of sacred garden spaces have long been recognized. Noguchi's first set (for Graham's ballet *"Frontier,"* 1935) established his working formula later applied both to sculpture and to landscape.

"I thought of space," he wrote, "as a volume to be treated sculpturally and the void of theater space as an integral part of form and action." The interior garden with sculpture at the Domon Ken Museum at Sakata, Japan, can also be seen as theater space and stage set. The same could also be said for the fountain setting in the small park at Costa Mesa, California, designed in 1980–82. Taking the discrete, individual work of sculpture as a point of departure, the artist envisioned both the metaphorical and physical possibility of frontiers of space opening out, embracing real land and concrete, where a walkable experience as in a garden was possible. The allegorical title of the ballet *Frontier* and the created landscapes or gardens as "frontiers" is not happenstance. For Noguchi, from this vision "would come a new consciousness free of the constraints set on art by the art market."

Even though the possibility of actually realizing the larger vision of sculpture as space outside the theater did not exist in 1935, it was the beginning of a long, productive period of studio experiments. Although many of these experiments in visionary space have remained models and a few have been cast into bronze sculpture, they were always conceived as projects to be ultimately realized by the artist. Noguchi could never develop a concept that was meant to remain only a vision.

In 1935, Noguchi met the architect Richard Neutra in Los Angeles and was asked by him to design the swimming pool for the Josef von Sternberg house. It was made in a plaster model and later cast in bronze, remaining a small bibelot sculpture. The pool's sculpted lozenge shape is smooth and stylish, representing an advanced free-form three years before Aalto designed the pool at the Villa Mairea. It would be interesting to be able to compare what Noguchi would have designed as an entire garden setting for the pool with Thomas Church's celebrated garden at El Novillero, where a similar pool was created more than a decade later.

In a series of sculpted playgrounds, beginning with one proposed in 1941 for Central Park, the hand of the sculptor carefully shaping and molding the earth is apparent, always managed with the controlled perfection of an artist working with studio clay. While the translation into full-scale garden space, where people actually move, would be far easier than the conversion of one-dimensional painting, as Roberto Burle Marx has done, it is difficult to ignore the sculptural quality of these playgrounds as objects one observes from the outside rather than something to be experienced in motion from within.

Between 1961 and 1966, Noguchi joined with the architect Louis Kahn to develop a most complex playground design to be built in Riverside Park in New York. Before it was abandoned by the Lindsay administration, several maquettes were created, from which it is apparent that although the space is molded and sculpted, there is an expansiveness and monumentality that leaves no doubt that it is landscape art designed for a particular site.

The sculpture garden at the Noguchi museum is a modest space, an extension of the museum galleries themselves, a setting for the artist's works in granite, basalt, and wood. Neither a neutral setting, like a sterile New York art gallery, nor a totally sculpted concept found in the playground projects, would have served the function of this garden. Here the artist has responded to the open sky, the trees and plants, in which the sculpture can live and mellow in the open air. The idea of nature growing rampant within the confines of a dull, flat piece of industrial wasteland while the stone and wood art works "age with wild exuberance" appealed to Noguchi's sensibilities. On the one hand it is a quintessential twentieth-century setting that could be in an anonymous rust belt section of any American city where nature has been reduced to tough ailanthus trees growing in back alleys. But Noguchi has not turned his back on this unsympathetic and denatured environment. Rather he has lowered fences and opened up views like a borrowed mountainscape in Japan, incorporating galvanized warehouses and transformer installations into the composition. "I bask in nature's confidence," he once wrote, but at the same time he remained able to receive compliments from man's decidedly unnatural, random, and inescapable intrusions which are somehow tamed by the artist's acknowledgement and acceptance.

Monument Valley Navajo Tribal Park

The enclosure and preservation of vast tracts of the natural landscape for public pleasure, especially in the western part of the United States, has been a landscape policy of incalculable importance. But a vast tract of land numbering hundreds of thousands of acres of wildness under nature's own curatorship stretches the definition of a garden or even a public park beyond all conventional understanding.

Yet the great American national parks like Yellowstone and Yosemite might, in their monumental yet accessible grandeur, extend definition beyond the merely domestic site or the public parks of urban centers. Our perception of the garden and extended parkland was shaped in the seventeenth and eighteenth centuries when the garden, as J. B. Jackson has pointed out, grew beyond its essential function of supplying food and medicine. "Now it became something much richer: a source of stimulation and knowledge and shared delight.…The garden became an almost sacred place; its seclusion and beauty, and the innocent sociability and work it provided, reminded many of earlier legendary gardens."[1]

1. Jackson, *The Necessity of Ruins and Other Topics*, p. 30.

This sacred quality Jackson identifies in the newly discovered "Gardens of Eden" or "Gardens of Paradise," as they were frequently called by those who fought for their public preservation in the nineteenth and early twentieth centuries, dominated the public park debate from the beginning. Not only aesthetic stimulation, acknowledgment of God's laws governing the universe, and the shared delight in the wonders of nature justified the public policy to endorse and protect this virgin land in the limitless stretches of the West. Health, domestic tranquility, and the sacred American "Pursuit of Happiness" that had been a part of the nation's manifest destiny would now be secured and celebrated in those gigantic public spaces, defined, tamed, and eulogized on a scale to match the collective ambition of conquest of the continent for the common good.

The act of identifying, enclosing, and preserving the natural environment for scientific study, moral uplift, and enjoyment, modified the landscape by man's intervention, a perfectly acceptable if somewhat truncated definition of a garden where scale or location or past history is not a differentiating element. There must be the element of intent. Gardens are a conscious intervention in the landscape and the national and tribal parks can be accommodated not only by the physical act of intervening but also by the conceptual act of observing and framing with our eyes these scenes that have been specifically selected and reordered by roads, overlooks, and viewing sites for that purpose.

The very name Monument Valley raises another question of definition, and again J. B. Jackson's discussion on its meaning in *The Necessity for Ruins* cannot be improved upon. "A monument can be nothing more than a rough stone, a fragment of ruined wall as at Jerusalem, a tree, or a cross. Its sanctity is not a matter of beauty or of use or of age; it is venerated not as a work of art or as an antique, but as an echo from the remote past suddenly become present and actual."[2]

In 1863–64, Chief Hoskinini led his beleaguered people into this valley for safety after Kit Carson had rounded up the Navajo in Canyon de Chelly. The valley's floor reaches an elevation of more than 5,000 feet and its status now as a part of a Navajo reservation identifies and protects the spectacular landscape. In the barren, windswept valley recalling a moonscape, a few Navajos raise sizable patches of corn, while others graze goats. It was not until 1959 that the Navajo Indian Reservation established the tribal park.

Roads dwarfed to thin ribbons of garden paths wind through the valley. At Monument Pass the road is bordered on both sides by monuments to be seen, admired, and exploited by photography, a common service provided by more conventional garden settings. The isolation of the place has been broken by this public twentieth-century intrusion and by camera setting off an endless chain of images. Familiarity bordering on the domestic strikes the viewer upon first seeing the natural sculpture of giant monoliths deposited during the Permian Period, recalling the valley's use as a set for John Ford's 1938 film *Stagecoach*. But in spite of this relentless intervention and public exposure, there still remains the "echo from the remote past" Jackson speaks of, in the Valley's isolation on the Arizona and Utah lines.

The man-made curatorship of this specific, monumental piece of nature, now communal real estate held in trust by the Navajo Tribe, declares for the nation that it is somehow special and has been set apart as nature idealized in the name of public policy and tribal memory. Roberto Burle Marx has said that a garden is nature rearranged into an ideal concept. The Valley has been carefully framed and identified by the roads laid out for the visitor's pleasure so that its natural beauty is indeed translated into monumental garden.

2. Ibid.

Bibliography

Adams, William Howard. *Roberto Burle Marx: The Unnatural Art of the Garden.* New York: Museum of Modern Art, 1991.

——. "What Makes a Garden?" Review of "Transforming the American Garden: Twelve New Landscape Designs," an exhibition by Michael Van Valkenburgh. *House and Garden* (March 1987): pp. 32–38.

Ambasz, Emilio. *The Architecture of Luis Barragán.* New York: Museum of Modern Art, 1976.

The American Renaissance, 1876–1917. Brooklyn, N.Y. : Brooklyn Museum, 1979.

Archer, B. J. , and Anthony Vidler. *Follies: Architecture for the Late Twentieth Century Landscape.* New York: Rizzoli, 1983.

Balmori, Diana, Diane Kostial McGuire, and Eleanor M. Peck. *Beatrix Farrand's American Landscapes: Her Gardens and Campuses.* Sagaponeck, N.Y.: Sagapress, 1985.

Bardi, P. M. *The Tropical Gardens of Burle Marx.* New York: Reinhold, 1964.

Barzilay, Marianne. *L'invention du parc: Parc de la Villette.* Paris: Graphite Editions, 1984.

Baumann, Ernst. *Neue Garten, New Garden.* Zurich: Girsberger, 1955.

Bayer, Herbert, Walter Gropius, and Ilse Gropius, eds. *Bauhaus 1919–1928.* New York: Museum of Modern Art, 1938.

Beardsley, John. *Earthworks and Beyond: Contemporary Art in the Landscape.* New York: Abbeville, 1984.

Blomfield, Sir Reginald. *The Formal Garden in England.* London: Macmillan, 1936.

Boesinger, Willy. *Richard Neutra.* Zurich: Girsberger, 1950.

Bottomley, M. E. "Landscape Design in a Modern Manner." *Landscape Architecture* 37 (January 1947): 43–49.

Built Landscapes: Gardens in the Northeast. Brattleboro: Brattleboro Museum and Art Center, 1984.

Brown, Glenn, ed. *European and Japanese Gardens,* Philadelphia: Henry T. Coates, 1920.

Brown, Jane. *The English Garden in Our Time: From Gertrude Jekyll to Geoffrey Jellicoe.* Woodbridge, Suffolk, England: Antique Collectors Club, 1986.

Bye, A. E. *Art into Landscape, Landscape into Art.* Mesa, Ariz.: PDA Publishers, 1983.

Byrd, Warren T., Jr. *The Work of Garrett Eckbo: Landscapes for Living.* Charlottesville: University of Virginia, 1987.

Byrd, Warren T., Jr., and Reuben M. Rainey. *The Work of Dan Kiley: A Dialogue on Design Theory.* Charlottesville: University of Virginia, 1983.

Church, Thomas. *Gardens Are for People.* New York: Reinhold, 1955.

Collins, Peter. *Changing Ideals in Modern Architecture, 1750–1950.* London: Faber and Faber, 1965.

Colvin, Brenda, *Land and Landscape.* London: J. Murray, 1970.

Contemporary Landscape Architecture. San Francisco: San Francisco Museum of Art, 1937.

Corbusier, Le. *Towards a New Architecture.* New York: Payson and Clarke, 1927.

El Novillero,
Thomas Church
(see pages 152–153)

Cranz, Galen. *The Politics of Park Design: A History of Urban Parks in America.* Cambridge, Mass.: MIT Press, 1982.

Creese, Walter L. *The Crowning of the American Landscape: Eight Great Spaces and Their Buildings.* Princeton: Princeton University Press, 1985.

Crowe, Sylvia. *Garden Design.* West Sussex, England: Packard Press, 1981.

Cutler, Phoebe. *The Public Landscape of the New Deal.* New Haven: Yale University, 1985.

Dal Co, Francesco, and Giuseppe Mazzariol. *Carlo Scarpa: The Complete Works.* New York: Rizzoli International Publications, 1986.

DeForest, Lockwood. "Opportunity Knocks!" *Landscape Architecture* 36 (October 1945): 10.

Deshouliers, Dominique, et al., eds. *Robert Mallet-Stevens, Architecte.* Brussels: Archives d'Architecture, 1980.

Dill, Malcom H. "To What Extent Can Landscape Architecture 'Go Modern'?" *Landscape Architecture* 22 (July 1932): 289–92.

Earle, George F. "Is There a 'Modern' Style of Landscape Architecture?" *Landscape Architecture* 47 (January 1957): 341–53.

Eckbo, Garrett. "Is Landscape Architecture?" *Landscape Architecture* 73 (May–June 1983): 64–65.

Eckbo, Garrrett. *Landscape for Living.* New York: Architectural Record, 1950.

Eckbo, Garrett. "Outdoors and In: Gardens as Living Space." *Magazine of Art* 34 (October 1941): 422–27.

Eckbo, Garrett. "Small Gardens in the City: A Study of Their Design Possibilities." *Pencil Points* 18 (September 1937): 573–86.

Engel, David. *Japanese Gardens for Today.* Rutland, Vt.: Charles E. Tuttle, 1959.

Fairbrother, Nan. *New Lives, New Landscapes.* New York: Knopf, 1970.

Frampton, Kenneth. "In Search of the Modern Landscape." In *Denatured Visions: Landscape and Culture in the Twentieth Century,* edited by Stuart Wrede and William Howard Adams. New York: Museum of Modern Art, 1991.

Garris, Laurie. "The Changing Landscape," *Arts and Architecture* 3, no. 4 (1985): 56–59.

Gebhard, David, and Sheila Lynds, eds. *An Arcadian Landscape: The California Gardens of A. E. Hanson.* Los Angeles: Hennessey and Ingalls, 1985.

Geddes, Robert. "The Common Ground," *Landscape Architecture* 73 (May–June 1983): 66–67.

Gintz, Claude. "Neoclassical Rearmament." *Art in America* (February 1987): 112.

Greber, Jacques. *Jardins modernes: Exposition Internationale de 1937.* Paris: Editions d'Art Charles Moreau, 1937.

Griswold, Ralph E. "To What Extent Has Landscape Architecture Been Modern Since the Renaissance?" *Landscape Architecture* 22 (July 1932): 296–99.

Groening, Gert, and Joachim Wilschke-Bulmahn. "Changes in the Philosophy of Garden Architecture in the Twentieth Century and Their Impact upon the Social and Spatial Environment." *Journal of Garden History* 9 (April–June 1989): 53–70.

Gromort, Georges. *L'art des jardins.* Paris: Vincent Fréal, 1934.

Gropius, Walter. *The New Architecture and the Bauhaus.* Translated by P. Morton Shand. Cambridge, Mass: MIT Press, 1965.

Hackett, Brian. *Man, Society and Environment.* London: Marshall, 1950.

Halprin, Lawrence. *The RSVP Cycles: Creative Processes in the Human Environment.* New York: Braziller, 1970.

Hines, Thomas S. *Richard Neutra and the Search for Modern Architecture.* New York: Oxford University Press, 1982.

Holmdahl, Gustav. *Gunnar Asplund, Architect.* Stockholm: Tidskriften Byggmastaren, 1950.

International Federation of Landscape Architects World Congress. *Landscape Towards 2000: Conservation or Desolation?* London: RIBA, 1979.

Jackson, J. B. *Discovering the Vernacular Landscape.* New Haven: Yale University Press, 1984.

Jackson, J. B. *The Necessity for Ruins and Other Topics.* Amherst: University of Massachusetts Press, 1980.

Jackson, Kenneth T. *Crabgrass Frontier: The Suburbanization of the United States.* New York: Oxford University Press, 1985.

Jellicoe, Sir Geoffrey. *The Guelph Lectures on Landscape Design.* Guelph, Ontario: University of Guelph, 1983.

Jellicoe, Sir Geoffrey and Susan Jellicoe. *The Landscape of Man.* New York: Viking Press, 1975.

Jellicoe, Sir Geoffrey and Susan Jellicoe. *Modern Private Gardens.* London: Abelard-Schuman, 1968.

Jellicoe, Sir Geoffrey, et al. *The Oxford Companion to Gardens.* New York: Oxford University Press, 1986.

Jones, E. Fay. "The Generative Idea." *Landscape Architecture* 73 (May–June 1983): 68–69.

Karson, Robin. *Fletcher Steele, Landscape Architect.* New York: Harry N. Abrams/Sagapress, 1989.

Kassler, Elizabeth B. *Modern Gardens and the Landscape.* New York: Museum of Modern Art, 1964.

Kaufmann, Edgar K., Jr. *Fallingwater: A Frank Lloyd Wright Country Home.* New York: Abbeville Press, 1986.

Kepes, Gyorgy. *The New Landscape in Art and Science.* Chicago: Paul Theobald, 1956.

Kiley, Dan. "Nature: The Source of All Design." *Landscape Architecture* 53 (January 1963): 1–27.

Krog, Steven R. "Creative Risk-Taking." *Landscape Architecture* 73 (May–June 1983): 70–76.

Krog, Steven R. "Is It Art?" *Landscape Architecture* 71 (May 1981): 373–76.

Krog, Steven R. "The Language of Modern." *Landscape Architecture* 75 (March–April 1985): 56–59.

Krog, Steven. "Whither the Garden?" In *Denatured Visions: Landscape and Culture in the Twentieth Century,* edited by Stuart Wrede and William Howard Adams. New York: Museum of Modern Art, 1991.

Lawrence Halprin: Changing Places. San Francisco: Museum of Modern Art, 1986.

Lux, Joseph August. "The Garden Beautiful." Reprinted in *Rassegna* (Bologna), no. 8 (October 1981), n.p.

Marx, Leo. *The Machine in the Garden: Technology and the Pastoral Ideal in America. New York:* Oxford University Press, 1967.

Mawson, Thomas H. "Retrospect and Prospect of Landscape Architecture in Britain." *Landscape Architecture* 7 (April 1917).

McGuire, Diane Kostial, ed. *Beatrix Farrand's Plant Book for Dumbarton Oaks.* Washington, D.C.: Dumbarton Oaks, 1980.

McGuire, Diane Kostial, and Lois Fern, eds. *Beatrix Jones Farrand: Fifty Years of American Landscape Architecture.* Washington, D. C.: Dumbarton Oaks, 1982.

McHarg, Ian. *Design with Nature.* Garden City, N.Y.: Natural History Press, 1969.

Meyer, Elizabeth K. "The Modern Framework." *Landscape Architecture* 73 (May–June 1983): 50–53.

Mindlin, Henrique. *Modern Architecture in Brazil.* New York: Reinhold, 1956.

Moholy-Nagy, Lásló. *The New Vision.* New York: Wittenborn, 1946.

Motto, Flavio. *Roberto Burle Marx.* São Paulo: Nobel, 1984.

Neutra, Richard. *Life and Shape.* New York: Appleton-Century-Crofts, 1962.

"New American Landscape" (seven-article anthology), *Progressive Architecture* 70 (July 1989).

"New Styles in Gardening: Will Landscape Architecture Reflect the Modernistic Tendencies Seen in Other Arts?" *House Beautiful,* March 1929.

Newton, Norman T. "Modern Trends: What Are They?" *Landscape Architecture* 22 (July 1932): 302–303.

Noguchi, Isamu. *The Isamu Noguchi Garden Museum.* New York: Harry N. Abrams, 1987.

Olbrich, Joseph M. "The Garden of Colors." *Rassegna* (Bologna), no. 8 (October 1981).

"Paysage" (nineteen-article anthology). *L'Architecture d'Aujourd'hui* 262 (April 1989): 32–89.

Pean, Prosper. *Le Nouveau jardiniste moderne.* Paris: Librarie de la Construction Moderne, 1929.

Pool, Mary Jane, ed. *Twentieth-Century Decorating, Architecture and Gardens: Eighty Years of Ideas and Pleasure from House and Garden.* New York: Holt, Rinehart and Winston, 1980.

The Princeton Journal, Vol. 2*: Landscape.* Princeton: Princeton Architectural Press, 1985.

Process Architecture [series]. No. 4, "Lawrence Halprin" (1978); No. 33, "Landscape Design: The Works of Dan Kiley" (1982); No. 46, "Landscape Design in Japan: Current Issues and Some Ideas" (1984); No. 59, "Creative Environment: Japanese Landscape" (1985); No. 61, "Landscape Design: New Wave in Califomia" (1985); No. 78, "Pocket Park" (1988); No. 82, "M. Paul Friedburg: Landscape Design" (1989); No. 85, "Peter Walker: Landscape as Art" (1989).

Purvis, Alexander. "This Goodly Frame: The Earth." *Perspecta* 25 (1989), p. 178.

Racine, Michel, Ernest J. P. Boursier-Mougenot, and Françoise Binet. *The Gardens of Provence and the French Riviera.* Cambridge, Mass: MIT Press, 1987.

Richard, Winfried. *Vom Naturideal zum Kulturideal: Ideologie und Praxis der Gartenkunst in deutschen Kaiserreich.* Berlin: Technische Universitat, 1984.

Rose, James C. *Creative Gardens.* New York: Reinhold, 1958.

—— "Articulate Form in Landscape Design." *Pencil Points* 20 (February 1929): 98–100.

Rykwert, Joseph. "Il giardino del futuro fra estetico e tecnologia." *Rassegna* (Bologna), no. 8 (October 1981).

Schermerhorn, Richard. "Landscape Architecture: Its Future." *Landscape Architecture* 22 (July 1932): 281–87.

Schildt, Goran. *Alvar Aalto: The Decisive Years.* New York: Rizzoli International Publications, 1986.

Sears, William R. "The Past and Future." *Landscape Architecture* 22 (July 1932): 288–89.

"Shades of Green" (three-article anthology) *Abitare* (March 1989) 272: 218–37.

Shepheard, Peter. *Modern Gardens.* London: Architectural Press, 1955.

Simonds, John Ormsbee. *Landscape Architecture: The Shaping of Man's Natural Environment.* New York: McGraw-Hill, 1961.

Sitwell, Sir George. *On the Making of Gardens.* London: The Dropmore Press, 1949.

Smith College Museum of Art. *Landscape Architects from the Cambridge School.* Northampton, Mass.: Smith College Museum of Art, 1984.

Snow, Marc. *Modern American Gardens Designed by James Rose.* New York: Reinhold, 1967.

Solomon, Barbara Stauffacher. *Green Architecture and the Agrarian Garden.* New York: Rizzoli, 1988.

Sorenson, Carl T. *The Origin of Garden Art.* Copenhagen: Danish Architecture Press, 1963.

Steele, Fletcher. *Design for the Small Garden.* Boston: Atlantic Monthly Press, 1924.

Steele, Fletcher. "Landscape Design of the Future." *Landscape Architecture* 22 (July 1932): 299–302.

Steele, Fletcher. "New Pioneering in Garden Design." *Landscape Architecture* 20 (April 1930): 159–77.

Tafuri, Manfredo and Francesco Dal Co. *Modern Architecture.* New York: Harry N. Abrams, 1979.

Thayer, Robert L., Jr. "Pragmatism in Paradise: Technology and the American Landscape." *Landscape* 30, no. 3 (1990).

Tischler, William, ed. *American Landscape Architecture: Designers and Places.* Washington, D. C.: Preservation Press, 1989.

Tomlinson, David. "Design in the Twentieth Century: Start with Art." *Landscape Architecture* 72 (May 1982): pp. 56–59.

Tschumi, Bernard. *Cinegramme Folie: Le Parc de la Villette.* Princeton: Princeton Architectural Press, 1988.

Tunnard, Christopher. *Gardens in the Modern Landscape.* London: Architectural Press, 1938.

——. *Man-made America: Chaos or Control?* New Haven: Yale University, 1963.

Van Valkenburgh, Michael. *Transforming the American Garden: Twelve New Landscape Designs.* Cambridge: Harvard University Graduate School of Design, 1986.

Voigt, L. B. "Modern Gardens." *Landscape Architecture* 42 (April 1952): 116–19.

Wesley, Richard. "Gabriel Guevrékian e il giardino cubisto (Gabriel Guevrékian and the Cubist Garden") *Rassegna* (Bologna) no. 8 (October 1981).

Wharton, Edith. *Italian Villas and Their Gardens.* New York: Century Company, 1904.

Wrede, Stuart. *The Architecture of Erik Gunnar Asplund.* Cambridge: MIT Press, 1983.

——. "Landscape Architecture: The Work of Erik Gunnar Asplund." *Perspecta* 20 (1983): 195–214.

Wright, Frank Lloyd. *An Organic Architecture: The Architecture of Democracy.* Cambridge: MIT Press, 1939.

——. *The Future of Architecture.* New York: Bramhall, 1953.

——. *Modern Architecture.* Princeton: Princeton University, 1931.

Zach, Leon Henry. "Modernistic Work and Its Natural Limitations." *Landscape Architecture* 22 (July 1932): 292–95.

Zagari, Franco. *L'Architettura del giardino contemporaneo.* Milan: A. Mondadori, 1988.

Index

Page ranges in **boldface** type indicate major discussions of specific sites.